Autumn Light

Autumn Light

My Fifty Years in Zen

Edwina Norton

Hamilton Books

Lanham • Boulder • New York • Toronto • London

Copyright © 2020 by The Rowman & Littlefield Publishing Group, Inc.
An imprint of The Rowman & Littlefield Publishing Group, Inc.
4501 Forbes Boulevard, Suite 200, Lanham, Maryland 20706
Hamilton Books Acquisitions Department (301) 459-3366

6 Tinworth Street, London SE11 5AL, United Kingdom

Library of Congress Control Number: 2020902790
ISBN: 978-0-7618-7207-8 (cloth : alk. cloth)—ISBN: 978-0-7618-7208-5 (electronic)

∞™ The paper used in this publication meets the minimum requirements of American National Standard for Information Sciences Permanence of Paper for Printed Library Materials, ANSI/NISO Z39.48-1992.

In this life, save the body which is the fruit of many lives.

Eihei Koso Hotsuganmon Sutra

Contents

Author's Notes

NAMES

The Buddha taught that all beings are interconnected and interdependent. We influence and are influenced by each other and by every experience we have. So it is that many beings, both intimates and authorities, have made it possible for me these past fifty years to follow the Buddha Way. In this memoir I use the real names of my family members with their permission. I use the *Dharma* names of my Zen teachers over the years and of friends who had roles in my ordination and Tassajara experiences. I use the real first names of friends from my early years of practice. I use fictional names for the two Tassajara monks with whom I came into conflict during practice period. I refer to the Tassajara practice leaders by their iconic role names—Abbess, Tanto, Director, Lay Entrusted Teacher, Shuso, Tenzo, Ino, and Jisha. Their influence on us monks was almost mythic.

BIBLIOGRAPHIC CITATIONS

Where possible, I have cited bibliographic sources for the Zen chants and verses I have quoted. However, much of Zen liturgy has been handed down over centuries and modified by different teachers. Where I can provide no definitive bibliographic sources, the chants and verses are those used by the Red Cedar Zen and San Francisco Zen centers.

Acknowledgments

I want to thank the many friends who over the years encouraged me in writing this book. One of them, writer Carol Yoon, gave my project an early, needed boost by referring me to writing coach Deb Norton (no relation). Deb introduced me to the "narrative arc" and pointed out the importance to my story of a vivid dream I had at Tassajara. Zen friends Bernadette Prinster read two early drafts and gave me kind and useful advice; and Carrie McCarthy generously offered to proofread the final manuscript. Life-long friend and scholar Ellen Dissanayake suffered through an early, rough draft, yet volunteered to review later versions and encouraged me throughout the writing process. Poet friend Luther Allen's criticisms made me realize some readers might question my story, so I added more information about Zen practice. For two years, Joan Connell, journalist, author, editor, and professor, guided me in organizing and polishing the manuscript. Her patience, knowledge, and encouragement were invaluable.

I also thank the Tassajara Zen practice period leaders, who gave me feedback on the manuscript sections pertinent to them. They appear in my story mostly in conversations with me or in dharma talks to the community. Although I use the convention of quote marks for these conversations, the leaders' words are *not verbatim*. Instead they are paraphrases based on the journal notes I kept during practice period. (As a kinesthetic learner, my habit is to write down what I am learning, to better understand and remember it.) All the leaders accepted my renderings of their presentations. My deep thanks go as well to former San Francisco Zen Center abbots Tenshin Reb Anderson and Zoketsu Norman Fischer for verifying my accounts of their teachings. Special thanks also to Red Cedar Zen Community guiding teacher, Nomon Tim Burnett, for ordaining me as a priest, for his resolve that I practice at Tassajara, and for reading my manuscript twice.

Finally, I am grateful to my sons, Alec and Dan, for their support of this project. They were intimately affected by what led me to Zen and what it has meant for my life. Without their kind permission, I would not have published this memoir. Lastly, I want to emphasize that this book is the story of *my* experiences and understanding of Zen Buddhism and Tassajara's practice period, *not* an authoritative or scholarly work. I extend to the reader the traditional apology the Head Student makes to the Zen assembly after answering their tough questions during the Dharma Inquiry Ceremony: "Friends, if my actions and words have misled you, please wash out your ears in the Dharma's pure harmonious silence. . . ."

Introduction

The Red Cedar Zen Community *zendo* in Bellingham, Washington is softly lit and unadorned. A small wooden altar at the front holds a gray, stone Buddha, a glass vase of fresh flowers, an incense bowl, and a large, flickering candle. On the bamboo floor, neat rows of square, black mats with round, black cushions placed on top announce that this is a place of order, serenity, and safety. The soothing light and silence invite us to be gentle with ourselves and each other. Entering, we select a place to sit and do a small standing bow to it before sitting down along with twenty-five other Zen students. A roughly equal number of men and women attend on Wednesday evenings, Red Cedar's primary weekly meeting time. Our ages range from early twenties into the eighties.

We sit cross-legged on a cushion or kneel on a bench or, with physical limitations, sit on a folding chair. We extend our spines to open our chests so we can breathe easily. We place our hands in the traditional Zen oval *mudra* against our lower abdomen, left hand in the palm of the right hand, thumb tips lightly touching. We take a few deep breaths and gaze softly toward the bamboo floor or the plain wall in front of us. The Zen tradition of facing the wall, not each other, reduces distractions, for we keep our eyes softly open in order to be awake to our surroundings. In this way *zazen* expresses our Bodhisattva vow to be available to help all beings.

The basic instruction for how to practice Zen is to "Just Sit" and observe what happens in the mind and body. No visualization, no mantra to recite. Just sit quietly and focus on the present moment. Eihei Dogen Zenji, the thirteenth-century Japanese founder of the Soto Zen tradition, the practice I follow, claimed that zazen is not the process of learning to meditate so one can become enlightened. It is the very *act of being enlightened*. That is, sitting zazen itself *expresses* enlightenment. This concept has profound implications, but it also can be read literally: Sitting in zazen opens (enlightens) the mind to a deep and broad awareness of reality.

In zazen, focusing on the breath helps calm the mind. Counting each exhale or inhale up to ten helps to focus the mind. Usually well before one reaches ten, one realizes the mind is thinking—about a difficult interaction earlier that day, an upcoming event, or a persistent worry. Students new to Zen are often surprised at how active their minds are (Monkey Mind) and even dismayed to discover how difficult it is to quiet down. This experience is natural. It is rare in ordinary life that we take time to sit still and observe the mind as we do in zazen. If one persists in sitting zazen, repeatedly letting go of thoughts as they come up, in time the mind calms down. Eventually most Zen students find their way to an alert but quiet mind.

It can appear to an observer that in zazen one is doing nothing, but the practice actually requires a very active engagement with both body and mind. To sit still yet energetically alert for thirty or forty minutes, one must pay close attention: "Did I just slump forward?" Sit up straight. "Oh, shoulders feel tense." Slowly, quietly shrug them. Hands have fallen open on thighs. Bring them back against the belly into the mudra. Pain in the knee is distracting. Breathe into it. Thinking about what happened last week. Return to just breathing in and breathing out. This patient way steadily trains the mind to relax and release repetitive, distracted thinking. This skill gradually carries over into everyday life, where one uses it to live in the present, be mindful, and respond with a clear head to whatever comes.

Zen practice is a study of the mind, how it functions, how it eludes reality, how it masks truth, and, with the right stimulus, how it can reveal to us important insights. Based on what we learn about and from our minds, we are guided by Buddhist teachings toward ethical, beneficial actions in the world. The mind works in a seemingly serendipitous way because we each are conditioned by many factors from the past and present. We are usually unaware of our deepest conditioning; our thoughts and actions are often unconsciously driven. Until we study our minds, our habitual actions can be, to a greater or lesser extent, outside our control. Through zazen, we can bring our attachments and delusions into awareness, where it is possible to release them, train ourselves in beneficial mental habits, help others, and live more happily ourselves.

Zazen can be calm and restful, but it is not an escape, as some believe meditation to be. At times when the mind is repeatedly distracted or frustrated or when one is in physical pain, it takes concerted effort and commitment to remain seated and still. Zazen reveals and reflects whatever is going on in our life, including unconscious material. In fact, zazen is a window into the unconscious. It informs us of negative emotions, beliefs, and perspectives we didn't know we had. What comes up during zazen can be disturbing, even alarming, but it helps us know ourselves in deeper ways than ever before.

Sometimes in zazen we encounter difficult emotional material we'd rather avoid. Maybe we're tempted to stop sitting and leave. This is when sitting in a group is helpful. We feel obliged to not disturb the other students, so we stick it out and observe what happens next. Not giving up trains the mind and body to be steadfast. Sometimes the group energy is high, joyful; other times it is heavy. Whatever the prevailing tone, sitting with others encourages dedication and right effort. We learn that everyone's effort helps everyone else practice.

In each period of zazen the mind offers up whatever is happening right now. The zazen experience is always unique because what's happening is always changing, often in unexpected ways. No matter the content or mood of one's zazen, the only thing one can do in zazen is to *be* with oneself as one *is*, in the *present*. Zazen trains us to be present—the only location where we can be fully alive. Working with the distractions of our worldly lives is the special challenge of lay practice, as compared to monastic practice, in which one spends much more time in silence and meditation and thereby is mentally freed to connect more deeply with the unconscious.

A daily practice of zazen at home can offer easier access to a quiet mind than sitting with the sangha once or twice a week. Sitting by oneself, one is not distracted by anyone else's energy, joyful or dark. Sitting at home at the same time of day every day, morning or evening, develops the habit of touching in with ourselves, calmly preparing for the day or winding down at its end.

Sesshins (retreats of days or weeks) combine the benefits of both individual and group practice. Following the rigorous sesshin schedule day after day is not easy, but doing so relieves us of daily decisions about what to eat, wear, or do. The mind is freed to become aware of habitual feelings and thoughts. Add to this freedom the unusual experience of living entirely in silence with others, and all manner of submerged thoughts, emotions, memories, and insights can become conscious.

Each of the three modalities of zazen—sitting weekly with sangha members, sitting at home alone daily, and sitting in sesshin for a week or longer—offers unique opportunities for training the mind. Each modality enhances the other two. Together they enrich and deepen the study of the self—which is, ultimately, to forget the ego-oriented self in order to be open to whatever is happening, moment by moment.

I learned to practice Zen in these three ways over time, beginning in the early 1970s. This was a few years after Suzuki Roshi had established San Francisco Zen Center, attracting a following of young Americans eager for the rigors of zazen. Because I lived fifty miles south of the city, I never practiced at SFZC, but I followed its entrepreneurial ventures—a downtown meditation center, two monastic centers, a bakery, and a restaurant. I also witnessed Zen's evolution from the Japanese strictly male institution to its gradual American inclusion of women as priests and ultimately as leaders. As a member of Haiku Zendo, the smaller center in Los Altos also founded by Suzuki Roshi, I enjoyed the relative serenity of our non-residential, lay practice (weekly meditation, dharma talks, study groups). However, I did not escape the influence of the masculine, institutional Zen tradition as it settled into the West. In fact, in those early years the warrior qualities of Zen helped me meet my challenging life circumstances with courage and determination. It was only in my elder years, when my physical stamina declined, that I began to question the spiritual benefit of Zen's warrior energy.

I was attracted from the beginning of my practice to books that suggested the simple teachings that guide me to this day: *Being Nobody, Going Nowhere* (Khema 1987); *Chop Wood, Carry Water: A Guide to Finding Spiritual Fulfillment in Everyday Life* (Fields 1984); and 9th century Chan master Lin-chi's description of the ideal monk as "a true man without rank" (Watson 1993, xxiv). These phrases expressed my longing to be truly, simply myself.

At age seventy-eight, after forty-five years of Zen practice, I was ordained as a novice priest (one in training to become a fully authorized priest who can ordain others). Now I wear robes—a black gown and a black *okesa* (Buddha robe) draped over the left shoulder. It is unusual to be ordained so late in one's practice, let alone in one's life. Usually the motivation to ordain is a calling to study deeply, perhaps to live monastically or teach in a Zen community, even to become a noted Zen teacher. These are appropriate goals for priests in their thirties or forties, who have many years of practice ahead of them. My ordination at nearly eighty would shape and limit the service I could offer the sangha in ways I didn't then anticipate.

Directly following ordination I was required to participate in an arduous, three-month practice period at Tassajara Zen Mountain Center in California. This intensive monastic experience demanded every ounce of my energy and determination, but it also awarded me, as my story reveals, insights into my life and early conditioning that I could not have had in any other way.

This book recounts events in my life that led me to Zen during its early years in America. Zen brought to the West a profoundly different understanding of the nature of reality from the Judeo-Christian view. Zen helped me understand and accept my life in an entirely new way. As a dedicated practitioner over many years, I have welcomed new people to the practice and helped them find their way in its multiple, exotic forms.

I am not an important person in Zen. I am not a charismatic teacher. I am a participant in and a witness to the flowering of Zen in America over the past fifty years. It is from this obscure but privileged position that I have recounted my life's experience in Zen Buddhism into old age and how it has inspired me. It is my hope that sharing my experience will encourage those who yearn to deepen their lives to venture out on their own journey—not only Zen students but also readers who in later life are drawn to Buddhist teachings. The trail of discovery is not always smooth. One can stumble over protruding, gnarled roots and hidden, inner rocks. But the trek is worth the cuts and bruises. The vistas along the way can be sublime.

Chapter One

The Journey Begins

Like many Americans attracted to Zen and other Eastern religions, I sought refuge in Buddhism from a difficult life situation. I was thirty-nine. Trauma in childhood had prepared me to *need* the equanimity of Zen and then much later in adulthood, once I found it, immediately to recognize its benefits. That childhood trauma distorted my understanding of myself and others for much of my long life. Buddhism regards distortion as a *delusion*, one of the three causes of suffering, along with *greed* and *hatred*.

The summer I turned thirteen, my dad noticed my back was crooked. I had inherited the same scoliosis that had caused my mother's back pain and weakness. Dad took me to his osteopath, who recommended an orthopedic doctor. Both parents accompanied me to the specialist, who examined my back and then took us all into a brightly lit exercise room. He told me to disrobe in an adjacent cubicle, removing everything but my panties, then return to the exercise room. There, he instructed me to push down my panties to just above the pubic area so that he could easily see my hip line. He said to stand in front of a mirrored wall, facing him, Dad and Mother, and a man with a big box camera on a tripod. I can still feel the hot flush of blood that blurred my vision as I stood, essentially naked, before Dad and the two strange men. I was mortified.

I stared at the floor so I wouldn't see the adults staring at me. I followed instructions to face first toward everyone, to one side, to the other, then to the mirrored wall, where I couldn't avoid seeing my nakedness. The photographer snapped pictures of all positions. A nightmare.

Afterward, Mother followed me back to the dressing cubicle where I burst into tears. "Why, what's wrong, dear?" she pleaded. I was mortified that she didn't understand how humiliated I felt, physically now a young woman, to be seen and photographed naked.

This was the first and most traumatic of many episodes in which well-meaning but ignorant people inquired about my condition as if my body were separate from me. "Oh! Look at that. Is it painful? Will it go away eventually?" I soon learned to disguise the abnormality as much as I could. I wore loose clothing, avoided turning my back to others, stood and sat erectly. I wanted to avoid being treated as an oddity. . . the monster I was convinced I had become.

I was measured for a brace. In a small, musty office at the prosthetics factory, again I was told to remove all clothes except for bra and panties. Again it was a man, a stranger, who examined me (with Mother present). The pale, near-sighted, gray-haired man was a little shorter than I was. He stood two or three inches away, stepping slowly around my body, measuring tape in hand. He placed the tape delicately on and around my upper chest, breasts, waist, hips, side chest, shoulders, front, and back. He stood so close that his sour breath washed over me again and again.

I was to wear the brace during all my waking hours. The only saving graces were that I did not have to sleep in it, and I could wear it under my outer clothing. I was grateful for the latter dispensation because it was an ugly contraption. Steel struts up the sides and back were attached front and back to a creepily skin-colored, leather-padded circle at the hips and padded slings for under the arms. The hip circle rubbed on my pelvic bones, and the arm slings chafed my armpits. Over time, I learned to shrink inward and upward to reduce contact with these parts of the brace. This compression strategy worked, but it also caused me to be chronically tense, and over time, anxious.

The brace was hinged in such a way that I could open and get into it, close it and, secured with some buckles, be entrapped in its rigid form. Its purpose was to correct and hold the spine straight, as presumably, I continued to grow, an outcome I think it achieved fairly well. It leveled and aligned the hips and extended the lower back so that the middle back became less laterally curved. But because it held the torso so rigidly, it prevented the spine from flexing naturally. I could bend forward from the hips, but if I curled forward from the thoracic spine, the padded arm slings poked out rudely from my back, making me look freakish. I was self-conscious about this when seated at my school desk, where I had to bend forward slightly to read or write. I learned always to remain upright, though this rigid posture was itself unnatural. I felt deeply ashamed to inflict the sight of me on my schoolmates.

I *was* grateful I didn't have to wear the ugly thing outside my clothing, even though worn inside, I looked twenty pounds heavier. At night, I hid the brace in the closet; it was unbearable to see first thing each morning. Later that school year, once I had learned the posture the brace created, I faked wearing it on mornings when Dad cooked breakfast. He didn't notice that I wasn't wearing the brace, and I got away with going to school without it for a couple of months. When I entered high school, I refused to wear it anymore.

At age thirteen I was like most adolescents, desperate not to be different. So navigating eighth grade in that ugly brace was a major test of character. The first challenge came in P.E. where we girls were required to "suit up," changing in small, individual cubicles that were curtained to protect our modesty. This was 1948, long before women's locker rooms were open and privacy no longer a priority. The doctor said I could take the brace off for P.E., but this meant I had to leave it in a changing cubicle. It was such an ugly thing, I was ashamed for anyone to see it. Miserable, I waited in a cubicle until the other girls had gone to the gym. When I came out, the teacher was nearby, and seeing my distress, she asked, "Why, what's wrong?"

I burst into tears. "I don't know how or where to hide my brace." She patted my shoulder and said, "You can put it in my changing room." I was so grateful to her for her understanding, which she quietly offered throughout that difficult school year.

That year the girls ostracized me. They taunted me with reports of slumber parties to which I pointedly had not been invited. They devoted entire "Slam Books" to me—stenographer's pads in which girls wrote anonymously what they thought of other girls. At recess they insisted that I read their mean remarks aloud while they stood around, snickering. They stipulated that I could have only one girlfriend at a time and appointed and rotated the girl every few months, ostracizing her too for the duration of her "term." I wondered at the time where that clemency came from. One of the leaders said, with sham sympathy, "Even you deserve to have one friend." I was so cowed by the gang's tyranny that I accepted whatever girl was selected as a "consolation friend." I hung out with her until someone new was appointed. I came to believe I deserved nothing more. After all, I was defective.

Days at school that year were a torture of taunts and humiliations, received and dreaded. I was grateful everyday for the final school bell that signaled escape to go home or on the city bus to my weekly piano lesson. My music teacher, a sensitive and artistic woman, never asked about school. But she no doubt could see how miserable I was, and she did her best to console me with Bach and Beethoven. I became devoted to her and to the piano. At home, Mother routinely asked me how the day had gone. When I could not report it had been fine, her only counsel, repeatedly, was to "Rise above it," advice that fell well short of my need for emotional support.

I don't remember what I told Mother about how the girls at school treated me. Probably I didn't reveal much. I didn't trust her. She had not intervened in the humiliating photo shoot at the doctor's office. Now I'm not sure what she could have done. In those days the medical profession knew little about the needs of adolescents. Patients (and parents) just did what the doctor told them to do. Plus, as I realized in psychotherapy many years later, Mother did not know how to interpret people's unspoken emotions. Born in 1900, she had been raised by two profoundly deaf parents along with seven boisterous siblings. She had no models for sensitively reading the feelings of others. Determined forbearance was the only legacy she could offer.

Having no one to whom I could express my gut-grinding panic and despair became the source of lifelong distortions about myself: My peers' rejection was entirely my fault and responsibility to rectify. I could not expect consideration from other people. These conclusions would adversely affect important decisions with regard to my future relationships and endeavors. Shouldering such grief and fear was a heavy burden to carry into young adulthood.

I did find emotional support when my parents became members of a Presbyterian Church and I went with them to Sunday services. The minister was a welcoming, loquacious man whose rich baritone voice was comforting as he delivered his sermons, chiefly on Christian ethics. His practical lessons on the Good Samaritan and the Prodigal Son, his disquisitions on Loving Thy Neighbor as Thyself and Turning the Other Cheek percolated in me as I tried to fathom my girl friends' cruelty.

Eighth grade was the crucible that shaped my behavior in relationships for nearly my entire life. When I suffered rejection, I struggled to rise above it—turning the other cheek. Though I often despaired of acceptance, because I believed in the Golden Rule, I never stopped aspiring to it. I could not believe my classmates could be so cruel just because I had to wear a brace. Hindsight suggests it may have been easier for me to feel confounded than to accept the shame I must have felt but suppressed.

I made it through eighth grade in one piece—at least physically. The psychological price I paid was that mentally I split off from my emotions. I separated my shame and confusion from my determined ambition to be accepted. I became two girls, one outwardly smart and seemingly self-assured, who could cope with rejection, and the other, inwardly crushed and fearful. This would be my strategy well into maturity, in fact, until I discovered Zen.

The next year when I went to high school, I was found perfectly acceptable and even sought after. The student body was about three hundred students from our town and a neighboring island, so the mix of students was both older and new to all of us. We freshmen were thrown back onto a level plane, each of us having to find our place among new students and teachers. In this larger context, we formed new alliances and roles, effectively ending the girl gang's power. They no longer dared to bully me publicly.

I enjoyed my classes and teachers. I joined several extracurricular activity groups—Pep Club, Ski Club, and Honor Society. I made new friends and started dating. By the end of freshman year, socially cushioned by this unexpectedly positive reception, I was elected one of three school cheerleaders. It seemed I was on my way, free at last from bullying.

The early summer between freshman and sophomore years passed quietly. I babysat, rode horseback, swam in Lake Washington and enjoyed the welcome Northwest summer sunshine. One evening in July I was babysitting down the street with the two little kids I often sat for. At dusk, I heard a knock at the front door. When I opened it, there stood eight or nine girls with mean looks on their faces—the gang from eighth grade. Among them were two girls I considered good friends that first year in high school. I asked what they wanted. They sniggered they were having a slumber party nearby (to which I hadn't been invited), and they thought they'd "pay me a little visit." They pushed their way into the house and stood around in the small living room, joking and poking each other. I asked them to keep the noise down so they wouldn't wake the children asleep upstairs.

Suddenly, several girls grabbed me, knocked me down, and started rubbing lipsticks on my face, neck and chest. I struggled, but more girls held me down and scribbled on my arms and legs. Panicked, with a surge of adrenalin, I wrenched free and vaulted into the nearby tiny bathroom, slamming and locking the door before they could follow. Trembling and sobbing, I gasped for air and looked in the mirror. I was covered with red and pink lipstick marks. What would the children's parents think when they returned home?

I spent the next half hour scrubbing the lipstick off with soap and a washcloth, shaking with fear and anger. When I could get no more lipstick off my now roughed and reddened skin, I put an ear against the bathroom door to hear what the girls were doing. Hearing nothing, cautiously I peeked out. They were gone and had left the front door wide open. I closed it and staggered into the den. Exhausted by the attack, I lay down on the day bed there and fell asleep.

Some time later—I don't know how long—I woke with a start to see the girls again in the house, surrounding the bed, glaring down at me. I had forgotten to lock the front door.

I leaped up from the day bed, pushed violently through the surrounding girls and dashed into the bathroom, locking the door. I sat shaking, trying to figure out what to do next. Soon, with loud taunts and laughter, the girls left again. Once I felt certain they were gone, I ran out, shut and locked the front door, and checked on the children upstairs. All was well.

I was in shock, drenched in shame. There had to be something wrong with me to have stimulated such fury. I couldn't tell anyone about the attack, not parents, not girlfriends. How to explain such an event? Even though I believed I did not deserve bullying, I feared some flaw of mine had invited it.

As I look back at that painful time, I wonder if Mother's counsel to "rise above it" was the very thing that perpetuated the bullying. Maybe my contin-

uing composure and uncomplaining response to their bullying had only further incited the girls. I could understand they might have been infuriated that
once in high school I was "safe" from further public humiliation. Thus, this
final private bullying session. Little did they know how fully defeated I
already felt. Or how, from that time on, I was convinced I was unworthy of
acceptance.

I had been consoled by my Presbyterian minister's sermons, but as I
matured, institutional Christianity's emphasis on the essential sinful nature of
humankind troubled me. Though I continued to feel undeserving as a person,
I couldn't define myself as fundamentally sinful. Hadn't I been punished
enough? I could not bear to be further denigrated. For the next twenty-some
years I rejected church going even though I longed for compassionate teachings, which ultimately I would find in Zen Buddhism.

I did grow stronger and more independent in high school. I listened more
to my heart and less to the dictates of peers, despite the lingering fear that I
might again be ostracized. I began to make important decisions independent-
ly. One of those was choosing to attend a different college from the one my
closest friends chose. Theirs was a better school than mine, but I needed to
start anew. Unconsciously I must have feared continuing to associate with
hometown friends. So I moved on. I became a very good student in college,
and I got a good education. The independence and determination I developed
the hard way in adolescence would enable me many years later to recognize
Zen Buddhism as my path, despite how different it was from my American
middle-class upbringing.

Chapter Two

A Family Tragedy

Fast forward thirteen years. After graduation from college, marriage to college sweetheart, birth of wonderful son, Alec, graduate school, unraveling marriage, divorce, single parenthood, dating and remarriage, second wonderful son, Dan, our family moves from Seattle to California. There I witness the richness and turmoil of the Sixties in the Bay Area: The Summer of Love, the Free Speech mòvement, the Vietnam War, and the transformation of bucolic Santa Clara Valley into high tech Silicon Valley. Struggling with an increasingly unhappy second marriage, I find myself at a turning point:

"Either I quit teaching high school or you and I get a divorce," I declared in a clear, firm voice. "I can no longer handle both you and a bunch of 15-year-olds."

It wasn't that I didn't love my husband, Dave. When we met I was immediately drawn to him physically and emotionally. I was captivated by his wit and dark humor, his wide knowledge of literature, music, and politics. He combined the steadiness and quiet assurance of my father with the intellectual acumen my education had taught me to appreciate.

Over the several years since we'd married, what I'd thought during courtship was social drinking had developed into a drinking problem, a serious one. I wasn't yet able to name it *alcoholism*. This was the late 1960s when people still thought alcoholism was a shameful character flaw, not a pernicious disease. But alcohol was seriously damaging him and us.

I'd tried to persuade him to control his drinking. I drank with him to encourage him to stop after a couple of drinks. I stopped drinking altogether in hopes he would stop, too. I repeatedly begged him to stop. When begging only made him devious, I looked for ways to work around his condition: I covered for him when he missed appointments and, occasionally, work. As much as possible I kept Alec and Dan (five years apart in age) out of his way to reduce the harm his bad moods might do them. He was never physically abusive to them or to me, but our family's emotional life grew increasingly chaotic. Over the fourteen years of our marriage, I had gradually assumed most of the responsibilities for our home and family. I became what is termed the *co-dependent* spouse. I unwittingly enabled Dave's addiction.

Two or three years prior to my ultimatum, in desperate moments, we'd talked about divorce. Because ours was a second marriage for each of us, we were reluctant to go that way again. There seemed to be no solution. He continued to blot out his unhappiness with drink, which only worsened what had become depression. I kept us afloat by being responsible for everything at home and working full time teaching high school English, a challenging livelihood for me. With both work and home life increasingly out of control, my own mental health was deteriorating. I began to withdraw. I looked drawn and depressed. I wore black a lot.

One Friday evening I had a moment of truth. Home from work, Dave appeared to be genuinely falling apart. "I don't know how I can face another day at work," he groaned, near tears. "I am so miserable."

I jumped in to rescue him again: "Let's get away for the weekend together. I'll stay with you the entire time, take good care of you, help you through this crisis."

He listened and paused. "Well, no. I thought I'd watch football on TV this weekend."

I felt my heart slam shut. TV football was something he watched every weekend. An inner voice addressed me loud and clear: "If you keep going like this, You. Will. Die."

I resolved to make some changes. Over the next weeks I considered the options. Then I delivered the ultimatum: I quit teaching high school or we get a divorce. I was still not addressing the real issue, alcoholism, but at least I was taking a step toward reclaiming myself. Dave argued that we couldn't live on just one salary. I said I would work part-time, perhaps teaching at community college. He resisted. I held firm. It was his choice: I stop teaching high school or we get divorced.

It took a couple months for Dave to believe we could make it on his salary if I worked some. "Okay," he said, "Quit teaching, but you should read Zen. It might calm you down." He was not a Buddhist, but he had majored in Far Eastern Studies in college, so he knew about Zen. Thus Dave provided both my most profound life problem, marriage to an addicted person, and its perfect solution, Zen practice.

As a co-dependent spouse I would do anything to solve our problems, including reading whatever Dave assigned. I began with *The Way of Zen* (Watts 1957). This did not change Dave, but it set in motion big changes in our lives because it brought me to Zen. Many years later I learned through

Buddhism that changing one's inner self actually is the only option for finding happiness.

I was puzzled but fascinated by the paradoxical concepts of Zen philosophy, exemplified in the enigmatic *koans*, ancient Zen teaching stories: What is the sound of one hand clapping? Does a dog have Buddha Nature? What was your face before you were born? Confounded, slowly I worked through Watts' book, taking almost a year to finish it. At times I could feel my brain physically scrunching as I struggled to understand ideas so different from those of my Western education. Ten years earlier, I had written a Master's thesis on the paradoxical poetry of John Donne. Perhaps that had primed me for Zen's inscrutability.

When I finished *The Way of Zen*, I wanted to learn more. In the early 1970s not many books on Zen were available in English for the common reader, but I did find *The Three Pillars of Zen* (Kapleau 1965). There I got a more concrete sense of Zen practice. From the book's illustrated instructions on how to sit zazen, I was inspired to try meditating.

I began sitting zazen for a few minutes a day in our bedroom where I could be away from the family. The book said to do zazen for thirty to forty-five minutes, but I was so agitated initially, I couldn't sit still for more than five minutes. After a week or so of daily sitting I worked up to ten minutes. Then for several days every time I sat in zazen, I became preoccupied with how I could redesign the clothes in my closet. I did quite a lot of sewing in those days, but it never occurred to me to recycle anything. Yet every day when I sat down for zazen, immediately I began to visualize one or another garment and how to remake it. Could I make that gray wool flared skirt into a pair of slacks? Should I shorten the leopard-skin velour robe Dave gave me for Christmas last year? After several daily episodes of this surprising obsession, I realized that what I wanted to redesign was not my clothes, but my life.

Three weeks into my tentative home practice, I was convinced I was not doing zazen correctly. I was so easily distracted by daily concerns, and my knees hurt sitting cross-legged. I needed instruction. That week I read in the local newspaper about a community college class on Zen Buddhism to be taught by a Japanese Zen priest. Excited by the synchronicity of my need and this opportunity, I signed up for the course.

I looked forward to this new experience, but I was anxious about venturing so far outside my conventional WASP upbringing. Since college I had leaned toward the disconsolate existentialist view of life as intrinsically meaningless. I had tamped down incipient longings for inspiration. Now in the early 1970s, desperate to improve an abusive home situation, I was willing to risk joining an exotic course on Zen.

The first evening eighty people showed up for the class, far more than the number of chairs in the room. I was surprised and reassured by this level of interest. Perhaps it wasn't such an odd thing to be doing. Sitting mostly on the classroom floor, we students eagerly awaited the teacher. Finally, several minutes late, a slender, young Japanese man with a shaved head swept into the room. He wore elegant, flowing black robes. A crisp white shawl collar accented his shining face. I was transfixed. This was Kobun Chino Sensei, just a few years in the U.S. and newly in charge of the Zen community, Haiku Zendo, in Los Altos. He would become my teacher—fulfilling the adage, "When the student is ready, the teacher will appear." His English wasn't so good, but even though I could understand only part of what he said, I found him magical.

Toward the end of the ten-week course, Kobun invited the class members to come for zazen at Haiku Zendo. By that time class attendance had dwindled to twelve or fourteen students. Three of us accepted Kobun's invitation. I found Haiku Zendo exotic—candles, black robes, tatami mats, mysterious wafting incense, bells, and two forty-minute periods of zazen—when at home I could sit for only a few minutes. Quite a challenge, but I was hooked. My two classmates and I went every Wednesday evening for several months. After each program, we three went out for coffee and talked excitedly about the experience. We were full of questions: "What was Kobun talking about when he said '*shikantaza* [just sitting] is not something you understand. It's indescribable'?" or "What did he mean by 'Sitting is pointless'?" His teaching was so mysterious. So wonderful.

Meanwhile, Dave, at home alone with the boys on Wednesday nights, was growing restive. He wasn't so comfortable with my foray into Zen. Reading about Buddhism was good—after all, he had recommended it. Being gone every Wednesday night at some weird zendo was—well, he didn't know. "What's happening to my little Presbyterian girl?" he teased, only half-joking.

I had stepped out of our domestic arrangement and was on the way toward saving myself and our children's lives. Regrettably, not his. I could not and would not turn back.

What was so compelling about Zen practice? The biggest attraction was Kobun. My initial impression of him on the first day of his class stuck with me. In his warm receptivity to us students, Kobun was quietly charismatic. He emphasized correct posture in zazen and sometimes came around to gently adjust our bodies. His light touch up my back was deeply encouraging. He spoke softly during his dharma talks, often humorously and usually haltingly as he searched for the proper English words. His Japanese accent and esoteric teaching style could be difficult to understand. He seemed to drift from idea to idea organically, rather than ordering his thoughts logically. It was like listening to beautiful music or watching a ballet dancer. One felt refreshed, uplifted; but afterward it could be hard to say what Kobun had actually said.

The Zen aesthetic entranced me, too, in its simplicity and Japanese design. Haiku Zendo was the former two-car garage of a ranch style home. The zendo's interior walls were white and unadorned. Wooden sitting platforms called *tans,* raised two feet above the floor, lined the four walls. On the tans, square, black pads called *zabutons* were placed edge to edge with a round black *zafus* for zazen in their centers. Japanese tatami mats covered the center floor area, topped by more zabutons and zafus for zazen. At the front of the zendo, also on a raised tan, were bells of different sizes, including a large one with a lovely deep tone. A simple wooden altar was in the center of this tan. On it were a Buddha statue, a large white candle, a votive candle, an incense bowl for stick incense, a wooden box for incense chips, and a vase of fresh flowers. The altar candles and incense were lit for zazen and for the chanting and bowing service that followed zazen. Bells were rung to start and end periods of zazen and to accompany bowing and chanting during the service. The teacher's seat was beside the altar, facing us. We students sat facing the walls in traditional Japanese Zen style. An entrancing and stately ceremonial world, far from the pain of my then unhappy daily life.

I loved the silence of zazen and the soft, soothing light. I could sit down and rest deeply in the quiet, alone, but in the reassuring company of others earnestly seeking peace and truth. I was humbled and grateful to be with Kobun and the other, more experienced Zen students. I could be safe in their presence. In this compassionate container, I learned to sit cross-legged, spine extended, shoulders and arms relaxed yet energetic enough to hold my hands at my lower abdomen in the Zen mudra. Eyes half open, I gazed softly at the wall.

As I learned the physical posture for zazen, I also learned to receive whatever thoughts arose. I trained myself to just observe whatever came up, however difficult or distressing. And let it go—over and over again. The zendo silence received and held me as I was, moment to moment. It permitted me to face life as it was. Sometimes I felt infused with the glowing candlelight as if I were alight with inspiration.

I became Kobun's student and Haiku Zendo became my refuge. There I could stop worrying about what others thought or what contortions I needed to go through to satisfy them. Some years later I told a friend, "I love to come to the zendo because I can just be myself. I don't have to pretend to be what other people want." Zen revealed the way out of the pain and chaos of my marriage. Zen practice remains, after all these years, my refuge.

It took only a few weeks for the settled quiet of zazen to present me with reality: The problem I had was not just that Dave drank too much. The problem really was alcoholism. When this bad news first arrived in my awareness, I fought it. This couldn't happen in *my* family. *I* couldn't have married an alcoholic. *My* husband was too intelligent and educated to be an alcoholic. I didn't know yet that a critical feature of the disease is self-delusion, which makes it so difficult to cure.

Every day when I sat down in the calm and steady container of zazen, the message persisted. Calmly, gently, it insisted that, yes, it was true: alcoholism was the root problem. Painful as it was, I knew I must accept this reality so that I could find a way to overcome it. The power of zazen is amazing. When we accept what is actually happening, we are freed to work with it effectively.

I set about problem-solving. In addition to sitting zazen every morning, I started going to Al-Anon meetings to learn what I could do to change the situation. There I learned the Twelve Step program that Alcoholics Anonymous follows. I also learned how I, too, could recover from the damage and turmoil alcoholism inflicts. How consoling it was to hear other people's stories, so similar to mine. For three years I attended two or more Al-Anon meetings a week, absorbing the steps to emotional recovery and beginning to reconstruct the way we lived. I talked to Alec and Dan, then ages fifteen and ten, about alcoholism and their dad, and what we all could do to change our situation. They seemed relieved to name the problem.

Dave still drank. I still shouldered virtually all responsibility for our family life and home. I worked around his increasingly dysfunctional behavior—failure to keep promises or appointments, criticism of almost everyone, procrastination, anger and bad moods, vociferous cursing. To shelter the boys from his distressing presence, I busied them in outside activities. Change was slow.

The sense of failure I had from not being able to solve the root problem of Dave's drinking, however, over time eroded my sense of personal agency. As he grew sicker and more miserable, he blamed and berated me more. In frustration and confusion, even as I practiced "Letting go and letting God," I came to half-believe that I was the cause of his unhappiness. Or more accurately, that I was responsible for making him happy, and I'd failed. This is the basic premise of co-dependence. It would distort all of my relationships for many years to come.

Dave claimed I didn't love him unconditionally as a good wife should. He criticized me for always Doing, never Being. I was a Zen student. Why couldn't I just sit still and Be? Why was I always Doing something? he repeatedly complained. He was not aware that because he did almost nothing to take care of our home and family, I had to do more. Nor did either of us realize that my constant activity was a symptom of anxiety and unhappiness. By the time I finally woke up to the emotional peril I was in, my sense of self had been seriously damaged. Like the proverbial frog that would have jumped out of the water had it been thrown in when it was already boiling, I was deep in the steadily heating water of co-dependence before I realized I must get out or die.

At last, supported by Al-Anon friends, I summoned the courage to tell Dave I thought his problem was alcoholism. As is typical in these situations, he denied the label, calling his problem depression—which did underlie and also perpetuate his drinking. It was many months before he could admit that he needed help. During that time, finding relief in the support I got through Al-Anon and zazen, I continued those practices. I grew stronger emotionally. Then one day Dave agreed to go to an AA meeting. Over the next year or so he was in and out of both AA and denial. We separated for a year. We reunited for another year. But he couldn't stay away from alcohol. We divorced and a few months later he died by suicide. The tragedy of my life is that though I was able to save myself, I could not save him. Nor could I prevent the emotional damage to my sons, a bitter legacy for a mother to leave her children.

The Buddha taught that when we cling to or resist reality, we suffer. Through Zen and Al-Anon I learned to face the suffering that addiction causes and over time to let my anger and grief go. The zendo and Al-Anon meetings were refuges from a difficult home life, but my lack of self-confidence infected even my Zen practice. I didn't know if it was appropriate to discuss personal problems in *dokusan* (private interview with the teacher), but when I met with Kobun my problems spilled out anyway. He was very kind, accepting me as I was. Mother had always wanted the best for me, but her advice usually focused on improvements I should make. My husband, in the classical dynamic of familial repetition, also counseled improvements, repeatedly saying I was wrong to feel what I felt. When Kobun simply accepted what I said I felt, it was a revelation. In one dokusan session I confessed that I was afraid of driving on the freeway with Dave, even though he was a good driver. Kobun said, "Of course. Your fear comes from the responsibility you feel for your children. You don't want anything to happen to you for their sakes." His acceptance amazed me. Those closest to me repeatedly had dismissed my feelings. Kobun's kindness became the model for how I wanted to treat others. I don't always live up to his example, but acceptance of others as they are remains my goal.

Three years into practicing Zen, one evening after a brief, face-to-face interaction with Dave, I intuited that he was going to die, though he was not then physically ill. He had come to our house because the next day he was moving back to his hometown in Washington. He had phoned to tell me this news, wanting to avoid the pain of saying goodbye in person. But young Dan insisted that he come over. Of course it was a sorrowful visit, but worse than that, I detected a blackness underneath the surface of his face, as if death was in him. After he left, I was badly shaken and couldn't sleep that night.

The next morning, alarmed by the power of my insight and not knowing what to do to help Dave, I phoned Kobun. I didn't know if it was proper for a student to call him at home, but I was frightened. Immediately, he responded:

"Yes," he said, "please come see me. I will help you prepare for his death." When we met, Kobun gave me very practical advice: Get my own affairs in order by making a will and family trust. Write a letter to Dave telling him that I forgave him and asking his forgiveness; and after that, phone him to re-establish friendly terms. Kobun's pragmatic counsel was all the more meaningful, given how unworldly he seemed to be.

I did what Kobun advised, and some months later, when Dave took his life, again Kobun was there for me. He came to our house and led traditional Zen ceremonies on the fourteenth and forty-ninth days after Dave's death, as is the Buddhist tradition.

Because of Kobun's compassion at this crucial time, I had good reason to be devoted to him. I felt blessed to be his student and trusted him completely. In the difficult time after the divorce but before Dave's death, I had asked Kobun if I could have a lay person's ordination, called *Jukai*. In this ceremony of commitment to Zen practice one receives and recites the Precepts, the ethical principles of Buddhism. Usually Jukai is performed for several students at once, but Kobun arranged for the ceremony for me alone. I believe he wanted to fortify me for the intuited, upcoming death of my husband. It was a wonderfully validating experience. I felt deeply honored and seen— like a bride. Kobun gave me the dharma name, *Shun Ko Myo Kuo—Spring Light, Wonderful Happiness,* to encourage me to believe there would be happier times in the future. I felt the ceremony was also for Dave, for it was he who had introduced me to Zen. As it turned out, Jukai occurred just two months before he took his life.

Chapter Three

A New Life

Now I was in fact a single parent, responsible for supporting Alec and Dan financially and emotionally while dealing somehow with the shock of Dave's suicide. I continued as Kobun's student. This provided stability and support, but my primary focuses became being sure Alec and Dan were okay and finding a job with enough income to support us. I didn't have time to grieve, let alone to deal with the guilt I felt over not saving Dave. In hindsight, I was overwhelmed by his suicide. I couldn't process it. It would take many years to work through the grief and anger generated by our divorce and his death.

The impacts on Alec and Dan were also complex, though different. As Dave's alcoholism worsened over the years, Alec oriented his life more outside the home. Dave had not been unkind to Alec, but to my distress, he had not been a nurturing stepfather and never legally adopted him as I had hoped. Dave's final abdication of filial responsibility must have underscored the disappointment I feared Alec experienced as he was growing up. His year of attending Alateen gave him some perspective about how little family members can do about alcoholism, so from high school onward he focused on his studies and his life outside the family. As a freshman in college 400 miles away, he devoted himself to his education. I supported him from afar as best I could, seeing that he had what he needed materially and encouraging him in his schoolwork and friendships. Summers he lived at home and worked as a lifeguard, and I could then support him more directly then. I worried that I didn't do more to help him deal with Dave's suicide, but he seemed to manage his life pretty well. In four years he graduated first in his college class and received a fellowship to study at Oxford University in England. For him, too, it would take years to work through the conflicting emotions our family experience created for each of us.

The first summer after Dave's death, I did arrange for both Alec and Dan to see a child psychologist so they could process their emotions. After a few sessions (which I was not allowed to attend), the therapist reported that she felt they had worked through their initial emotions and could discontinue therapy. Perhaps because I did not want to interfere with their process, I never initiated any discussion about concerns they had about my responsibility in Dave's death. That might have helped all three of us. I was dimly aware that I wasn't doing as much as was needed, but I didn't know how to address our grieving as a family directly.

Dan, fourteen and the "only child" now that Alec had returned to college, suffered more deeply. He was attached to his father and being still quite young was strongly impacted emotionally. Not only did he have to absorb the bewildering tragedy of the suicide, but also because now I had to work full time, I was no longer at home after school to nurture him. However, I had a brainstorm. I contacted the Big Brothers and Sisters organization and engaged a volunteer, Bob, a systems engineer, who became Dan's Big Brother for three years. He took Dan on frequent camping trips to California's national and regional parks, teaching him many outdoor skills. They also rebuilt our old VW Bug's engine. This project gave Dan the initial skills to become a talented mechanic during high school and college and later to own and manage a car repair and tire business in Colorado. Dan benefited greatly from Bob's guidance and big-hearted moral support. He eased Dan's way through his teenage years and thereby greatly helped me in parenting.

During these years when the boys were in high school and college, I worked full time, moving strategically from job to job to develop a satisfying and well-paid career as a management and organization development specialist. All three of us were intently pursuing our interests, so there seemed little time to review or integrate the emotional calamity of Dave's death. I regret that I didn't help the boys more to process their feelings. Instead I supported each of them in pursuing their interests. In this way, I acted more as a father, the parent who bridges the child to the world, than a mother, who provides a loving refuge.

During this time at Haiku Zendo I joined the sangha board of directors and worked on the capital campaign Kobun had initiated to acquire a larger center. Over two years we raised almost three hundred thousand dollars but fell short of the amount needed to buy the Japanese-style mountain house we wanted. Eventually we used the money to purchase both a retreat center in the Santa Cruz Mountains (Jikoji) and a city center in Mountain View (Kannon-do). In the midst of this expansion, Kobun suddenly announced he no longer wanted to lead our sangha. Instead, he would become a traveling teacher. We were shocked. He assured us we were quite capable of practicing on our own. I remember puzzling over what that might mean for me. I knew only the traditions of sangha life and following the teacher. I was just learning how to develop a new career and be a single parent. How could I, who had come to depend on Kobun, take full charge of my Zen practice as well?

There was much consternation and discussion among Kobun's students. A few refused to let him go and followed him to his new locations, first in Santa Cruz and later in Taos, New Mexico. I owed Kobun a profound debt of gratitude for his kindness to me. I knew the Buddhist tradition was to do as the teacher asks. After weighing the sorrow I felt at losing him against all he had done for me, I decided I must do as he asked. I must let him go. Now I was more on my own than ever. The next years were ones of intense personal, spiritual, and professional development for me as well as for my children. As it turned out, Zen practice and the opportunities it offered to understand my life supported me well as I went forth in the world.

When Kobun was still at Haiku Zendo and I was sitting zazen daily at home, my life had gradually stabilized. I began to feel stronger and calmer. I had found refuge. Daily zazen instilled in me the determination, discipline, and courage needed to face life's challenges. Among them was the legacy of negative emotions from my adolescence onward—guilt, fear, shame, anger, resentment, loneliness. Zen practice would slowly heal me.

Six or seven years into practicing Zen, however, I still doubted that I was doing zazen correctly. This uncertainty probably expressed the deep lack of self-confidence I had learned in adolescence. Also, though I read voraciously in Zen and Buddhism, I began to realize I did not clearly understand the teachings. They were so different from Western culture's logical, dualistic perspective. At the zendo I memorized and chanted the Heart Sutra, the mainstay of Zen practice, but I didn't understand much of it: "Form is emptiness, Emptiness form." What does *emptiness* mean? How could *form* and *emptiness* be interchangeable?

I sat zazen in half lotus for forty-minute periods, but I couldn't tell if my disorganized mental activity meant I was letting go of thoughts or I was just agitated. I deeply loved zazen and bowing and being silent with others, but I couldn't articulate what I experienced in zazen or why. It seemed dream-like—the quiet zendo, the incense and bells, the bowing. Even as I was devoted to zazen, I still doubted myself. I did not understand it at the time, but I had begun to enter the unconscious mind of broader awareness that zazen offers. Zazen had begun to guide me.

One evening sitting zazen, I had the powerful insight that my spiritual understanding would be slow to develop. Observing how quickly a sangha friend was progressing along the path toward priest ordination, I recognized my practice was halting and hesitant, despite my devotion to it. I visualized myself sitting zazen on a pile of rocks—stolid, enduring, but slow to advance. This insight called to mind an image that had struck me a few years earlier. In a Zen study group we learned about "skillful means," the ability of the Buddha to teach even the most deluded person. Kobun told us such people were called *icchantika,* a Sanskrit term from which the English word *enchanted* was derived. Icchantikas were beings who greatly desired enlightenment but were considered incapable of it. They were enchanted or benighted (though the Buddha could teach them). The word icchantika reverberated through me. Yes, that was my condition. For an assignment to write an autobiographical poem in a class I was taking then, I wrote about this condition. I described myself as a "blind being, enchanted stone, unwilling to be saved." I felt I had been enchanted by my early conditioning and later my traumatic marriage. My path to awakening would be long.

I sorely missed Kobun, but his absence did not lessen my commitment to Zen. I joined Keido Les Kaye to practice at Kannon-do. Les was a good teacher, ordained by Suzuki Roshi; Haiku Zendo had been in his garage. At Kannon-do I began more deliberately to study the basics of Zen practice— How to work more subtly with the body and mind in zazen; what the correct forms were for kinhin, bowing, chanting, and moving in the zendo. I favored teachings about the simplicity of Zen practice. *Just sitting, Nothing special,* and *Non-gaining* were Zen watchwords that steadied me. During this period of recovery from family trauma, I also benefited from the many resources of the 1980s Human Potential movement in bloom in California. I read voraciously and attended workshops on how to recover from emotional co-dependence, on assertiveness training for women, and on adult development. All good medicine. I was healing.

At home I sat every morning at six a.m., facing the brick fireplace in the living room. A simple clay Buddha statue from a friend in Sri Lanka presided from a nearby bookcase. On Friday mornings a neighbor joined me in zazen. Royce was a college psychologist, a lanky, exuberant, and kind fellow a few years older than I. He didn't want to belong to a Zen group but was delighted to sit zazen once a week together. He rode his rusty bike to my house, arriving just before six a.m. I left the front door unlocked so he, and occasionally one or two other friends, could enter quietly to join zazen.

Hosting weekly zazen in my home stretched me emotionally. I was still very much a beginner at Zen but powerfully drawn to share the wonders of zazen. I relished the generosity that welled up in me when others quietly entered my living room to sit. Initially, a frisson of fear also rushed up my spine when I couldn't see who was entering because I was facing away from the door. Yet sitting together silently seemed to protect the space. The Buddha statue that I bowed to, the candle and incense that I lit before morning zazen made the room seem inviolable—even sacred. In fact, non-Zen friends often commented about my home's calm atmosphere. Integrating Zen practice into daily life helped my healing. Royce and I sat together on Fridays for nearly twenty years.

During these years I also began to study the foundational teachings of Buddhism, the Prohibitory Precepts and the Eight-Fold Path. Somehow, perhaps because when I started practicing, American Zen was still developing, I hadn't been guided to study these basic teachings in any depth. Kobun and Les had strongly emphasized *just sitting* and *non-thinking*. Devotional practices had not yet been encouraged, except perhaps at the major Zen centers.

I loved the teachings on ethics and beliefs because of their usefulness for living in the world. Perhaps my Presbyterian minister's sermons years before had established ethics as my spiritual bent. In my career in the corporate world as an organization consultant and trainer, I advised and taught company managers about communications with employees. Daily I had the need to apply the teachings on ethical behavior. Especially pertinent to both work and personal life were the Buddhist Precepts of not lying, not slandering, not being possessive, and not harboring ill will. Every day, organizational life brought opportunities to test myself in one or more of these prohibitions. Working with them as spiritual practice was fortifying. Likewise, the Eightfold Path steps of Right Speech, Right Action, and Right Livelihood were beacons. Right Livelihood ultimately guided my decision to leave the defense contract firm where I worked. I could no longer in good conscience support managers responsible for manufacturing instruments of war. I was slowly awakening. Buddhist teachings guided my life.

I began to penetrate the meaning of the Buddha's initial teaching, the profound and original Four Noble Truths. The first Truth is that suffering (dissatisfaction) is a fact of our human life. Life isn't all or only suffering, but we repeatedly experience some form of suffering. The second Truth is that suffering has an identifiable origin, the human habit of having preferences for the way we want things to be. The third Truth is when we know what causes suffering, we can end or at least reduce it. And the fourth Truth is that the Eightfold Path shows us how to accomplish this.

The Four Noble Truths percolated in my interactions with work colleagues, friends and family members. When I had a conflict with someone, I began to notice that my mind seized on explanations for a behavior of theirs I didn't like or understand. I saw I was skilled at analyzing their possible motives, and I used my "story" about them to feel safely in control. As I continued to practice Zen, though, I saw that these deft analyses of other people left me feeling separate—safe, but alone, even alienated. Plus I spent a lot of time justifying why I should avoid or manipulate these "foes." Eventually, I saw that this was the work of the second Noble Truth—the origin of suffering, which is, simply, that we suffer because of the way we *think* about our experience: We grasp and cling to experiences and phenomena we desire, and we push away those we don't want. Whichever reaction, cling or reject, we perpetuate our unhappiness.

To work deeply with this second Truth, I had to delve into the foundational Buddhist concept of *No Self*. Because all phenomena, including ourselves, are always changing, nothing has any permanent or abiding characteristics or nature. Psychologically, this teaching is difficult to accept. Our minds behave as if we are permanent. We have memories, histories. It feels like we are the same person we've always been. Early in my study of Zen I had acknowledged the deeply non-Western concept of No Self, but I did not understand it. Now I began to see how it was the assumption, itself, that was the cause of my suffering: Especially when circumstances made it necessary for me to change my ideas or actions, I suffered from not being able to stay as I was. So the belief that I was one "thing" was what caused me to suffer.

If I was always changing, what or who was it that demanded that things be the way "I" wanted them to be? If I gave up believing "I" existed in any way other than transitorily, I saw my desires and aversions were absurd. They should drop away as I naturally focused on responding to what actually was happening in the present. Learning this teaching and developing the habit of applying it has taken many years, but finally I can understand the Buddhist saying of Seng-Ts'an, Zen Patriarch (Sixth C.): "The Great Way is not difficult for those who have no preferences." (Seng-Ts'an).

Still, I stumbled over self-centeredness and its many cravings and aversions. Perhaps because I understood that change was the nature of life, now I began feeling restless in my job. I considered a change of livelihood. I investigated returning to teaching; I took some night classes on the Rudolph Steiner educational system. I explored other parts of California where I might live and work. Eventually, I gave up on making a big change and simply resigned from my corporate job to go into business as an independent organization consultant. During the five years that I worked for myself, I gained personal agency, new professional experience, and skills for living life more creatively and contentedly.

I continued my daily home practice of zazen, sat weekly at Kannon-do, and took part in sesshins. Over these years I gradually gained access to my suppressed, early conditioning. I recognized my strong tendency to rescue people, the co-dependent habit I had perfected when married. I realized I gravitated toward people who needed support but could not offer support in return (I married two of them). I realized that avoiding intimacy may have been a hedge against being rejected by others—no doubt a habit I had established in adolescence.

Chapter Four

Abundant Inspiration

In the early 1990s I learned of a job teaching English at a women's university in Okayama, Japan. I had the requisite academic credentials and experience. I had twenty years of Zen practice, which included some knowledge of Japanese culture. I thought living in Japan might shake up my thinking as I had been wanting. I applied and got the job. I was fifty-seven.

Before leaving for Japan, I heard about the Rinzai Zen monastery, Sogenji, located in Okayama. Sogenji was a training center whose Abbot, Shodo Harada, welcomed European and American Zen students. Once in Japan and settled into teaching, I visited Sogenji and met the Abbot. I spoke with him about becoming a guest student during the university's summer vacation. When I formally applied in writing, he granted me permission.

I was delighted but a bit nervous about this opportunity. I had participated in many week long sesshins, but I had never lived in a monastery, much less one in Japan. Also Rinzai Zen was reputed to be more rigorous than Soto Zen, plus I knew I would be handicapped linguistically. (I didn't have to know much Japanese to teach at the university, which hired English-speaking teachers to improve students' pronunciation.) Monastic practice would be a challenge. I hoped it would increase my confidence as a Zen student.

Most Sogenji monks spoke English, but the services, ceremonies, and Abbot's talks were all in Japanese, so at first I felt bewildered about what to do and where to go. The schedule was challenging—awakened at 3:30 a.m., to bed at 9:00 p.m. with days full of zazen, ceremonies, and work tasks. For the first two weeks my back and legs ached from long hours of sitting and rushing to keep up with the other monks. After that my body adjusted. I needed only the twenty minute nap after lunch that all the monks took to get through the long days. Being able to follow the rigorous schedule would give me the new confidence I sought.

It was a privilege to live amidst the graceful beauty of Sogenji's 350-year-old structures and gardens, first built in the early Edo period. One entered the monastery by a long walkway up through ancient pine trees from the residential street on which Sogenji was located. The monastery's classical, two-tiered Buddha Hall at the center of the compound greeted the visitor. Its two tiled roofs and majestic, curved eaves bespoke both serenity and power. Inside the cavernous Buddha Hall every morning from 4:00 to 5:00 a.m., we monks sat and chanted in Japanese. We chanted so rapidly it took me two weeks to get my tongue around all the syllables.

This daily hour of rapid, full-throated chanting was invigorating. Afterward, we processed silently downhill to the zendo for zazen. On my first morning, once we were settled on our zafus, a bell was rung, and, thinking it indicated the start of zazen, I was startled when everyone leaped up and ran out of the zendo. Bewildered, I followed as quickly as I could, back up through the woods to a spacious room between the Abbot's apartment and the Buddha Hall. There we sat and waited to be called for *sanzen*, the daily private interview with the Abbot. Later I learned that the monks ran to be sure they would get to speak to the teacher. This racing was a monastery tradition but actually not necessary because the Abbot saw everyone every day. I learned to run too but never fast enough to be first in line. My best was to be second, once only.

The resident monks each worked on a koan with the Abbot. As a visiting monk, my daily sanzen consisted instead of the Abbot demonstrating the powerful, slow breathing technique of *sussokkan* to calm and focus the mind. Following my sanzen, conducted mostly in silence as I knew little Japanese and the Abbot, little English, I enjoyed the solitary walk back down through the woods to the zendo for more zazen.

There were many aesthetic pleasures to enjoy at Sogenji: Outside my room at 3:50 a.m. each morning, I relished the exuberant stars in the black sky as I waited to join the other women monks and walk arm-in-arm up to the Buddha Hall. On rainy mornings, I found equal pleasure walking huddled under umbrellas, large raindrops spattering on ancient granite steppingstones. And each time we entered the dark, cavernous Buddha Hall, a tiny thrill of fear energized me.

Later, after morning zazen, I enjoyed bustling from the zendo in tight formation with the other monks to crowd before the kitchen altar. There we chanted a fast and guttural, possibly animist, chant, to the "kitchen god" before entering the dining area to sit at a long table for our *oryoki* meals. Though I never knew the meaning of the chant, its primitive energy cheered me.

The resident monks rotated daily as *tenzo* (cook). A second monk acted as assistant cook. Several times I was allowed to be assistant, washing rice and chopping vegetables. I was amazed at how fast the tenzos worked to cook three meals a day for twenty-five people. At day's end I followed the tenzo in ritually closing the monastery. In the dark at 9:00 p.m. we walked the entire compound, striking two wooden clappers (*hyoshigi*) together sharply and shouting an ancient incantation to ward off any evil spirits lurking on the grounds. It was spooky, especially as we scooted by the graveyard to enter the furthest, dark building, the Founder's Hall, where intruders conceivably could be hiding. I had to laugh: middle-aged and still afraid of ghosts.

The monastery week offered many sensory pleasures. During zazen in the zendo, which was located next to the graveyard, I was soothed to hear the occasional splash of water, the hollow clink of watering cans, and the swishes of bamboo brooms as neighborhood family members faithfully cleaned the graves of their ancestors. Once every five days when we monks had a partial day off from the normal schedule, I luxuriated in the monastery's wooden hot tub (heated by a wood fire) in the bathhouse with the other women. On summer evenings, I relished sitting zazen as twilight softly turned to night. On a few nights at dusk in August I was astonished to hear bullfrogs in the Zen garden pond clear across the monastery compound "throat singing" in two deep tones, like Tibetan monks.

Both the aesthetics and the practice at Sogenji were rich culturally and spiritually. I enjoyed finding my way in Rinzai Zen practice and into friendships with monks from Japan, Europe, Australia, and the U.S. After my summer residence, I was permitted to attend several seven-day sesshins throughout the year. I also stayed at the monastery some weekends. I have many good memories of Sogenji and Japan, one of which relates to my mind's development.

Participating in monastic practice, as well as living in Japan with only the most rudimentary literacy, did have the effect I had wanted. Experiences intensely different from what I was used to shook up my mind. Before moving to Japan, I had been warned about "culture shock." Though I read several descriptions of this phenomenon, I could not have imagined the actual experience. On three occasions during that year in Japan, one at Sogenji and two in my teaching life, I experienced culture shock.

These episodes were characterized by mental confusion that built up over a few days concerning particular situations in daily life and work. One was about my sophomore English students' behavior. They wouldn't speak in class. I tried many ways to get them to talk, but they refused. I concluded that their resistance meant they did not like me. Only at the end of the year did I come to understand: they did not want to disappoint me. Their resistance was out of respect.

At the crisis point of this and the other culture shock episodes, I realized I had absolutely *no idea* what was going on. My brain felt both clogged and dizzy. I couldn't relate cause and effect. On the surface, things appeared to be understandable, but in the state of culture shock, for a few hours I felt intensely confused. I observed activities and analyzed their meanings from my Western perspective, but my analysis completely missed the boat. My mind whirled, I couldn't catch my breath. I had no process for sorting things out. I just had to capitulate to not knowing. It was humbling—and enlightening. The antidote for an episode of culture shock was simple and at hand: I just needed to talk to another American or European who had lived in Japan longer than I had. With their support, in an hour or so, my frenzied mind would calm down. I would see the humor in the experience; I felt cleansed, like my mind had been rinsed. I had come to Japan to shake up my thinking. This was the shaking.

Being functionally illiterate in Japanese gave me new respect for immigrants finding their way in new countries. Being illiterate also made it necessary to fall back on an unconscious awareness I didn't know I had. For example, I could find my way to and from locations even though I couldn't read street signs or understand the directions I asked for when taking the bus or train. It was harrowing to feel lost, but apparently my unconscious mind recalled the details for getting to and from where I wanted to go and staying safe, for I always found my way.

These "peak experiences" of culture shock had the additional benefit of boosting my self-confidence. When I returned to California a year later, I felt able to make several major life changes. I did not return to corporate work but found jobs in the nonprofit and education worlds. I did not return to Zen practice at Kannon-do but participated in a variety of meditation groups—a Vipassana group in Palo Alto, which introduced me to retreats at newly established Spirit Rock in Marin County; two different Tibetan Buddhist groups in the San Jose area and their associated retreats. Most importantly, I found Tenshin Reb Anderson of San Francisco Zen Center, who would become a significant teacher for me.

Reb's ability to elucidate the mysteries of Buddhist thought was remarkable. It was from him that I first learned about the Buddhist teachings on the co-arising of all phenomena, a fascinating description about how the mind works: Phenomena exist for us in the way they do because we bring our preconceptions to them. As a product of Western dualistic thinking, I had never questioned that reality exists "out there" and that my task was to perceive and understand it as best I could. If my understanding differed from that of others, I usually concluded that I was wrong or confused.

But Reb described perception as a mental process of matching current experience with previous experiences: Our senses and brains respond to sounds, sights, smells, etc., based on our unconsciously stored memories of similar or identical phenomena. We first perceive and then immediately identify phenomena we encounter, such as bird song, apple tree, lavender. In this way, we bring our prior experience to each current sensory experience. In doing so, we actually *co-create* our experience.

We add to this basic recognition and identification of an object our emotional associations with it. For example, when we feel warmth toward a person new to us, our positive feeling may arise from unconsciously associating him with someone we loved in the past. Or when we fail to recognize someone who greets us, we have not called up or perhaps ever stored a memory of that person from a previous encounter. In this way, our conscious and unconscious brains work with our senses to form and shape our present experience. As Reb explained it, a split second before we become consciously aware of a sound or a smell, etc., unconsciously we pre-select what and how we think about it based on our unconscious storehouse of past experiences. In fact we select for conscious acknowledgement only that which we recognize from past experience. Of course, this perception mechanism can also perpetuate misunderstandings we never corrected, potentially causing us no end of trouble.

The idea of co-creation was electrifying. I can still picture myself in the cavernous, candle-lit zendo at Green Gulch, listening with fascination to Reb's words. I could not then quite grasp how co-creation worked, but the truth of it resonated in me. Its implications were thrilling: If our brains actually help shape the phenomena we experience, we have more influence on its meaning to us than I had realized. And thereby more ability to relieve our suffering. Reb's teaching, I later learned, was based on the third century work of Buddhist psychology called the Abhidharma. I looked for books about this but did not find anything until ten years later when I read *Understanding Our Mind* by Thich Nhat Hanh. It describes a similar process as the unconscious "seeding" of our perceptions (Hanh 2006, 23-33). I have since learned that Theravadan monk Bhikkhu Bodhi has translated an Abhidharma resource (Bodhi 2003).

Contemporary neuroscience findings about how human brains work corroborate these ancient Buddhist teachings. Our unconscious pre-selection processes shape our experience of reality. Starting late in the first decade of the 2000s, some ten years after I first learned from Reb about co-created perception, developments in magnetic resonance imaging technology began to yield scientific insights into how the human brain works. Books for the lay audience about brain function began to appear. I intuited that this information might help me better understand Buddhist teachings about the mind, and I eagerly read everything I could find.

A book particularly important to me was *The Master and His Emissary.* In "Part One, the Divided Brain" (McGilchrist 2009, 15-209) I learned that our left brain hemisphere (termed *The Emissary*) contains our conscious mind, which produces and controls language. It performs many important functions to insure our survival, such as finding and inhabiting shelter. The left brain analyzes, categorizes, and thinks abstractly; it has a sequential, linear approach to reality. It deals in facts, uses denotative language. It pins things down, makes them clear, precise, fixed. The left hemisphere seeks control over the environment. It wants to be in charge and because it is conscious, it usually seems to be.

The right hemisphere (*The Master*), conversely, is largely unconscious. It is the storehouse of our previous experiences, the "seeds" Thich Nhat Hanh described, upon which we draw to identify and understand our present experience. The right hemisphere lacks vocabulary, but it accesses and inhabits the land of relationships, of the individual and of the ever-changing, evolving, and interconnected "*between-ness*" of things/beings (McGilchrist 2006, 95, 97). The right hemisphere "knows" that we exist only in terms of and through our encounters with other beings and things—the very insight of the Buddha. The left hemisphere is concerned with survival of the individual and seeks to dominate self and other. The right hemisphere's forte is the broad awareness of and connection with other beings. Empathy and emotional understanding are largely right hemisphere functions. It appears that the insights of Buddhism into the interdependence of phenomena arise from our right hemisphere, whereas our persistent self-centeredness and desire to be in control, our penchant for having preferences, and our resistance to change arise from our left hemisphere.

This information about how each of our brain hemispheres operates was life changing for me. It revealed faulty thinking patterns I had developed over a lifetime. The tension between the two hemispheres explained the difficulty I often had in believing the direct experience I accessed through my intuitive, right hemisphere—the kind of understanding one can have in zazen. I saw now that I habitually doubted my natural insights. When I sensed something but could not articulate it, my cognitive, verbal left brain jumped in, commandeered the nonverbal insight, and put it into language that wasn't always sufficient to represent what I felt or knew intuitively. Instead of crediting my intuition, I discounted what I couldn't articulate. I didn't trust it. I didn't trust myself.

I had acquired this habit of self-doubt from my earliest years in part because I was repeatedly told, directly and indirectly, that the way I felt or thought about things was not right. "Don't be so sensitive," Mother repeatedly urged. "You're always Doing. Why can't you just Be?" my husband complained. Implored to be different, I learned to doubt what I felt. When I sensed that a person was angry or fearful but claimed he was not, I routinely discounted my insight. In general, I persistently doubted my own judgment. How miraculous to discover, then, that though I might not always be able to verbalize my understanding, I actually could rely on it as *my* experience. This new information about the brain enabled me at last to trust the deep and broad awareness that zazen makes available. My beloved teacher Kobun had been acting from this knowledge when, to my amazement, he accepted what I told him was true for me.

I was excited that contemporary neuroscience helped me better under-stand the Buddha's teachings of twenty-five centuries ago, teachings I be-lieved but had found hard to apply in my daily experience: If all phenomena are empty, co-dependently arising, and without separate, abiding nature, as Buddhism teaches, then everything, including ourselves, is continuously changing. It is impossible to cling to or push away something that is always changing. But because it still appears to us that things, including ourselves, are permanent or ongoing, we do cling and push away. And we suffer. We feel dissatisfied, frustrated (or hurt or afraid or grief-stricken) because we forget that everything is changing. Forgetting, we become attached to what we want and refuse what we don't want. Either way, we (our left brains) suffer from not getting what we want.

The Buddhist teaching is that since clinging and pushing away are what cause us suffering, we must relinquish both being attached to what we desire and resisting what we don't desire. We must live in the immediate, present moment, without attachment. Accept that we and all phenomena are in flow. Know that pleasant will soon turn to neutral or unpleasant and back again. Grasping and pushing away are pointless. Worse, they perpetuate our mistak-en belief that we are separate from our experience and can control it.

In January 2001, I had an experience that catalyzed a major change in my life, both spiritually and logistically. It came about during the three-week January *practice period* at Green Gulch Zen Monastery that Reb led. The previous July, I had retired at age sixty-five from fund raising at Santa Clara University. I was free to pursue my heart's desires, chief among them Zen practice, especially at Green Gulch. I loved the gently sloping terrain and the fresh ocean breeze of this headlands farm and monastery. The walk down the long driveway through aromatic eucalyptus trees into the quiet monastery compound was a meditation in itself. For this retreat I had the additional good fortune to be billeted in the Japanese hexagonal wooden guesthouse. I couldn't have asked for more a restful and inspiring accommodation.

Glowing with gratitude for this good luck, I found my room, which I would share with another woman, and began unpacking. As I put away the few items of clothing and equipment I had brought, I discovered that I had forgotten to bring my *rakusu*, the bib-like ceremonial garment given me by Kobun at my Jukai ceremony in 1977. How could I have forgotten to pack it? It was almost as dear to me as my children. I believed it essential for doing sesshin practice. Could I even sit without it? How would anyone know I was a serious Zen student? It was my Zen identity. . . . Ah, I realized, this was Ego speaking. Was this an opportunity to practice forgetting the Self? I was ashamed to feel this ego-attachment, but I also felt a little naked without this "badge" of commitment.

As practice got underway, I mourned the absent rakusu. How could I have been so un-mindful as to forget to bring it? Finally I wondered, Why did I forget it? Was it time, perhaps, to let go of Kobun? It had been twenty-five years since I was his student. Maybe I should be moving on. I mused on this possibility for a few days. At the end of the first week, I had dokusan with Reb. I told him about forgetting the rakusu and how upset I felt. I shared with him the speculation about needing to move on in practice. I considered Reb my teacher now (a few years prior he had accepted me as such). Could I sew a new rakusu and receive from him a new dharma name? In effect, could I have a second lay ordination? After some consideration, Reb said he would be happy to give me the Precepts. I was thrilled. Kobun had given me a Japanese-made rakusu, but the San Francisco Zen Center tradition was for students to sew their own. Green Gulch had regular sewing classes about the exacting sewing process. I could take the classes that spring. At Reb's suggestion, I would also do an art project about the Precepts while sewing the new rakusu.

During the spring and early summer, I drove several times up through heavy San Francisco traffic to Green Gulch to get help cutting out and sewing my new rakusu. Back home after each lesson, I carefully sewed the pieces together. I also studied *The Mind of Clover* (Aiken 1984) about each of the ten Grave Precepts, the ethical guidelines of Buddhism. After reading about each Precept, I assembled my art supplies—charcoal paper and colored pastels. I sat in zazen for twenty minutes or so contemplating a Precept's meaning and noticing the feelings and images that arose about it. Then I painted an abstract design for the Precept. I enjoyed accessing the unconscious awareness available through zazen to evoke my relationship to each Precept. Sewing and painting: two lovely, nonverbal, right brain expressions of Zen practice.

In August Reb officiated at the Jukai ceremony at Green Gulch. He asked me to lead the procession of fifteen students receiving the Precepts. Always nervous about ceremonial roles, I was reluctant, but I did as he asked. Despite performance nerves, the ceremony inspired me. Reb gave me the dharma name *Zaren Shinge,* meaning *Sitting Lotus, Deep Understanding.* I cherished this opportunity to rededicate my practice and looked forward to continuing to practice as Reb's student.

Then 9/11 happened. Along with the entire country, I was shocked and frightened. I pondered its meaning and effects on my life. I had been thinking of leaving California, but I was thankful I was still in my home of nearly forty years where I felt safe. Concerned for future terror attacks and always anxious to be prepared, I took classes in emergency preparedness through my city. That November I did what would be my final sesshin with Reb. Then the following summer, after the annual reunion with seven college friends in Washington State, I took the advice of a Zen student I had met at Green

Gulch to check out the city of Bellingham. I knew it had a Zen group with an excellent visiting teacher, Zoketzu Norman Fischer, a former San Francisco Zen Center abbot.

I toured Bellingham, found that in addition to the Zen center, it had an Iyengar yoga studio and a good swimming pool, two other requirements for my health and happiness. I liked the size of the town (then 60,000) and its beautiful setting on Puget Sound, now called the Salish Sea, with the Cascade Mountains visible to the east. Although I didn't know anyone there except that one Zen acquaintance, I decided this was the place for me. I returned to California, sold my house, and moved to Bellingham, all within three months. I was eager to begin anew. My only regret was that I would no longer be able to study with Reb.

Fortified by nearly thirty years of Zen practice in various settings, I was ready for a new adventure. Thanks to Kobun's gentle encouragement in my early days to be myself, to the fortifying experience of Rinzai practice in Japan, to Reb's brilliant teachings on the nature of mind (and eventually to neuroscience's discoveries about the human brain), slowly I was gaining solid footing in Buddhism and life.

Chapter Five

A Maturing Practice

In early November, I said goodbye to my long time home in Santa Clara, California and got on the road to Bellingham, WA, a snowstorm at my heels as I sped northward over Siskyou Pass. I knew no one in this Northwest college town, but at age sixty-eight, I had more confidence and enterprise than ever before.

It was the right decision. Within two weeks of arrival I was sitting zazen with the Bellingham Zen Practice Group at its meditation space downtown in the old Masonic Hall. The Zen group shared the second and third floors of this 1905 building with three other Buddhist groups—Shambhala, Insight, and Mindfulness. Each group had one weeknight for its meditation program plus a few weekends for retreats cooperatively scheduled throughout the year.

The Zen group had been established in 1991 by a handful of Bellingham Zen students in their middle to late twenties who sat zazen together in their homes and offices. They included Nomon Tim Burnett, now our sangha's Guiding Teacher, whose enthusiasm for practice made him its natural leader from the beginning. Over the years, Tim trained at Green Gulch and Tassajara and in 2000 was ordained as a priest by Zoketsu Norman Fischer. Norman was Founding Teacher of the Bellingham and Vancouver B.C. Zen groups, where he led sesshins from 1993 onward. Our sangha, renamed Red Cedar Zen Community in 2007, was and remains a lay practice group. It is non-residential, financially supported by members chiefly from the local area. Our programs, events, and facility are maintained entirely by volunteers. When I joined, the active sangha was small, twenty or so members. They used all the correct forms for zazen, bowing, chanting, services, and sesshins that I had experienced in thirty years of Zen practice in California and Japan. I could slip right in, take a seat, and begin contributing to the sangha.

Tim was welcoming and quickly found volunteer opportunities for me, first among them managing the quarterly sangha newsletter, which we produced on computer, photocopied, and mailed to one hundred or so interested recipients. In this role I worked with other sangha volunteers as well as with Tim, who generated most of the newsletter information. My colleagues were educated and independent people but apparently little experienced in teamwork or collaboration. Our communications and progress were frequently halting and frustrating. Gradually I came to understand that we were on a long learning curve about how to work together effectively. Learning to communicate well would take several years.

My background in organization development helped me understand that groups go through stages of development. One model (Tuchman 1965) describes the stages as *Forming, Storming, Norming, and Performing*, each with its particular challenges. I arrived in the Bellingham Zen group toward the end of the "forming" stage and the beginning of the "storming" stage when we would need to work out goals, roles, and responsibilities. There were disagreements about how to operate and what tasks belonged to which roles. After about seven years, we did move into the "norming" stage. There we could establish policies and procedures and figure out how to share the many tasks needed to keep our practice and organization running smoothly. Development of our sangha became a long-term focus for me. My goal was for all the tasks needed to make our organization work well to be assigned to members. That way everyone would have a stake in our success.

By 2007, we felt we had outgrown the Masonic Hall and began to look for other locations. We found a place just a block away. It was a 1930s building with an unfinished interior we could modify to meet our needs. We signed a lease and began to finish the interior. We built walls to create a lobby, a library, a small meeting room, and two bathrooms, leaving a larger space for the zendo. We painted all the walls and ceilings (several times) and installed bamboo laminate flooring. Members and personal friends pitched in money, labor, and expertise to finish the building interior. The Insight Meditation group agreed to sublet from us and share in the monthly lease. After five months of hard work and hundreds of volunteer hours, the building was habitable. On our last Wednesday evening at the Masonic Hall, we walked at dusk in solemn procession up the hill to our new home, carrying our Buddha statue and small wooden altar and ringing our ceremonial bells.

As we grew in membership to about eighty by 2019, the need for structure and role definitions also grew. Over time I had several organizational roles—outreach coordinator, membership coordinator, building rental manager, board secretary, board president—as well as practice roles for sesshins and some Wednesday nights—Tenzo, Ino, Doan, Jisha, Retreat Manager. Other senior members also rotated through these essential roles. Working with Tim and the Board, I wrote up policies and procedures—Tenzo notebook on kitchen procedures, communications and conflict resolution guidelines, sub-contractor agreement, sub-lease document. In consultation with attorneys, I drafted rental contracts for outside users of our building, and performance standards and review processes for our spiritual director. Helping the sangha develop organizational norms was my chief contribution to Red Cedar Zen. This work was often behind the scenes, and though sometimes I wished it were more obvious, I felt a deep satisfaction in helping to nurture our development.

As I settled into my new life in Bellingham, I found the city encouraged civic participation. I had always wanted to be a community volunteer. Now was the opportunity. I helped form a new neighborhood association and began attending city meetings. During this same time I was wondering about priest ordination. In dokusan with Norman when he came to Bellingham to lead sesshins, I discussed my ambivalent interest in priesthood and also my enthusiasm for civic work. He suggested that I think of myself as a "monk in the world," one who practices the Bodhisattva vow in worldly affairs. That way I could serve both interests. I followed his wise advice and volunteered for city boards and commissions. I became president of a neighborhood association. I served for four years on a commission that evaluated and recommended land for city parks. I spent four years on the city's Planning Commission. During these years, I also volunteered for Hospice as a massage therapist. Through volunteering, I made friends throughout the city and had the satisfaction of having a full life in the world, as well as in Zen practice.

Priest ordination continued to beckon me. I reflected on why I hadn't been able to take this step earlier. Years before when practicing at Kannondo in California, I had seriously considered becoming a priest. I envisioned wearing flowing black robes, appearing serene and wise, admired by friends for my dedication. I imagined how poignant it would be to shave my head, forsaking life as a woman. Gradually I realized I was romanticizing a serious commitment. I didn't know what priesthood was actually about, but I knew enough to see it was not the ego trip I was indulging in. I put these extravagant speculations aside.

Years later, in my seventh year practicing with Red Cedar Zen, Tim and Norman invited me to be *Shuso* (head student) for our winter six-week practice period, the annual time of intensified practice. The Shuso teaches classes on a Buddhist practice or concept, gives dharma talks, meets for tea with individual Zen students, and at the end of the practice period, takes the featured role in the traditional, public Hossenshiki Ceremony (sometimes called Dharma Combat). In this ceremony, the Shuso sits before the gathering of sangha members and responds spontaneously and, she hopes, penetratingly, to dharma questions.

I felt honored to be Shuso but afraid I was not up to the task. I feared the Hossenshiki ceremony, certain I could not respond adequately to the questions. Over the weeks of practice period, however, the role offered many opportunities to "speak my truth" to a greater extent than ever before—to step forward, as Tim described it. It took courage, but I found that when I appeared more fully, to my surprise, I was warmly received. Being Shuso continued the slow healing from the emotional damage I had incurred in adolescence and marriage.

One of the talks the Shuso gives is called a "Way Seeking Mind" talk about how she came to Zen and what experiences she has had in practice. A couple of years earlier I had given such a talk tracing my long history in Zen. I didn't want to repeat it. Instead I wanted to talk about a current life problem I was struggling with, a fading relationship with my adult sons. Preparing this topic would be a way to explore and understand my life in terms of the Buddhist teachings about *renunciation*, *home leaving*, and *acceptance* of things as they are—all tasks of the Zen monk.

Over the previous ten years, an emotional distance had grown between me and each of my sons, who were both now entering middle age. They were the most important people in the world to me, and I was bewildered and increasingly dismayed that we were becoming estranged. When they were children, I loved being a mother, having responsibility for their lives. I could count on their love, a precious gift in my bleak marriage. Now both lived far from me, one in South Dakota, the other in Florida. Email and phone calls were our best means of communication. In recent years neither called nor wrote often, even though I asked them to—first gently and then more urgently. Puzzled, I reflected on the time since they had left home. For the first twenty years of their adulthood, I was quite well connected to them, visiting each several times a year wherever they were living—California, Boston, Austin, Colorado. But as the 2000s wore on, our contact fell off. They were busier, their responsibilities for their families and careers greater. Naturally their lives took precedence over their relationship with me, but I felt miserable about the emotional distance between us.

I traveled to visit and talk with each of them. I asked them if they were harboring anger at me over incidents in their childhoods. They each claimed not. Of course, much of their childhood had been spent in the emotional chaos of alcoholism. There was no physical abuse, but there was dramatic behavior and strife, so I knew they were not unscathed. Most of all, I realized that Dave's suicide must have had an incalculable effect on them. Although thirty years had now passed since that dreadful event, I still did not know how to speak with them about my own complex feelings, let alone encourage them to explore theirs with me. I had failed them in this. Even so, I wanted them in my life and I wanted to be in theirs.

Both sons listened to my appeal but ultimately said they just couldn't find a way to be closer to me. Their lives were full of responsibilities. They didn't have time or energy to "tend" to me as well. Rationally, I understood this. When I was in my forties, my life, too, was crammed with endeavors and responsibilities. Still, I was unable to accept that we were no longer close.

I searched our family history to better understand how this estrangement had happened. I believed I had been a good mother—at least a "good enough" mother— in D.W.Winnicott's consoling definition of the parent who fully supports the child in infancy and then at the right time supports his gradually increasing independence (Winnicott 1971, 10-11). I was confounded. Of course I realized that Alec and Dan knew me and suffered from my faults as no one else could or did—as all children of parents do. They probably had sufficient reason to be wary of the "adult friendship" I was urging. As I examined this disappointing outcome further, I realized that each of them was a devoted parent. It was clear that they loved their children just as much as I had loved them when they were growing up. Some of the love they showed their families had to have come through me to them.

My wounded heart softened a little. Facing the facts of their situations, I felt somewhat relieved about my habitual fear that I was the sole cause of the distance between us. This new understanding didn't eliminate the loss I felt, but now I could see that there were more factors involved in our relationship than my strong attachment to them. I could recognize as well that as a person I was not anywhere near as important to them as they were to me. I could accept that this might be a natural shift between adult children and their parents. These insights reduced the sorrow I felt, though they did not eliminate it altogether.

As I was trying to process this disappointment, I was working as a volunteer massage therapist for hospice patients. I witnessed that it can be very hard to give up one's life. One hospice patient was a friend I had met through other volunteer work. I was able to spend some intimate time with her as she approached death. She was an intelligent and thoughtful woman whose husband had died unexpectedly two years earlier from a rare cancer. Now she had a different, rare, inoperable cancer. During our time together, she spoke quietly of her sorrow at losing her husband and confided in me about her own dying. She was very brave, working hard at accepting her coming death. She expressed her gratitude for her two adult children and the good life she had had. But the day she was told that she had only two or three more days to live, she was overcome with grief. There was nothing unresolved with her children, but accepting that she would die so much sooner than she had thought was overwhelming to her.

Witnessing this wrenching grief, I reflected on the estrangement from my sons. What if I died estranged from them? Would I be able to consider my life worthwhile? Knowing I had not persuaded Alec and Dan to change, I realized I'd better work on changing myself. Perhaps if I changed how I thought about our relationship, it would improve. Although I didn't consciously realize it then, according to Buddhist teachings, changing oneself *is* the only real option.

I sought counseling in the form of cognitive therapy, which asks the patient to examine negative or dysfunctional beliefs and substitute more realistic and positive ones. In therapy, I looked at and began to change how I thought about my role and relationship with Alec and Dan. During several months working with the therapist, I examined my beliefs and expectations, reported to her in our sessions, and received guidance on what to address next. Initially I found I couldn't easily reframe my thinking. Before I could shift it, I had to deal directly with my resistance, skepticism, and my own strong emotions of grief, anger, despair.

In the past when I had a problem my ordinary mind couldn't solve, I had discovered that if I sat in zazen with the determination to gain insight into a vexing problem, a solution eventually would appear. I decided to apply this approach. Through zazen awareness, I discovered the underlying reason why I wanted to be closer to Alec and Dan: I believed a "good relationship" would indicate that I had been a good mother and therefore had led a good life. When I saw this unconscious false reasoning, I knew I needed to figure out how to feel good about my life irrespective of my sons. This was not an easy task, but it was an essential one I had been blind to.

Over four or five months, I worked intensively. I examined my self-talk. I reframed beliefs that were negative and unconstructive. I managed to penetrate a whole network of misconceptions and negative conclusions about myself and others. This focused examination was often emotionally painful, but it was exciting to observe my mind changing. I was reconstructing a more realistic view of my life and relationships with Alec and Dan, as well as with others.

For one thing, I came to realize that each of us had become quite different people from who we were in earlier years when we were all three closely bound together. This was no surprise when I considered it objectively, but I hadn't understood it before. I came to the realization that maybe I could no longer define myself as a mother, the one role I had relished and assumed I still had. I had given up numerous roles—a mate, a professional (when I retired), a horseback rider, a skier. But not mother. Once a mother, could one ever not be one? This identity crisis also led to questioning my Zen practice. Why had it not been sufficient to sustain me through estrangement from my sons? Why, after so many years of practice, was I still struggling so fundamentally? Just then a book came to my rescue.

For many years, I have been blessed with receiving the right teaching *just* when I've needed it. Witness Kobun's appearance when I most needed acceptance and guidance. Now as I was confronting painful questions about my core identity, Vipassana teacher Rodney Smith's *Stepping Out of Self Deception* appeared. The book spoke directly to the problem: "Suffering is the desire for more choices than reality offers" . . . and "an awakened life depends upon addressing 'the pain of being me'" (Smith 2010, 49).

The pain of being me. Yes, I was in pain, emotionally separate from those I loved most. When we focus on maintaining our conditioned sense of self as we have been, we feel separate and alone. But feeling separate, Smith says, has no more reality than a feeling. I might not actually be disconnected from Alec and Dan. I might just *feel* I was.

Smith's teaching stabilized and inspired me to stop clinging to the now outdated idea of mother. His further insight revealed another bargain I evidently had made: Holding back, not being wholehearted in Zen practice or in life. To encourage readers to give fully to their lives, Smith wrote, "[W]hat we renounce in Dharma practice is a partial heart, because such an unresolved presence is an incomplete embrace of the moment" [where liberation is found] (Smith 2010, 76). I had long lacked the confidence to do something challenging. In the early days of practicing Zen I was afraid to participate in sesshins. Later I couldn't decide about ordination. I saw now that habitual hesitation had kept me from wholeheartedness.

I regretted having a partial heart, even felt ashamed of it, but I recognized it was an essential feature of mine—perhaps the "essential pain" of being me. I must practice with it. Lack of self-confidence and fear of criticism for years had made me anxious when trying new things: about being Shuso, about priest ordination. It's true that becoming a Zen student in the mid-1970s represented a big leap outside the mainstream norms of my youth. Stepping out of the protected, middle class milieu took some initial daring, but typically I proceeded cautiously. This caution forestalled the emotional liberation Zen offered.

I saw now that only I could save myself. Alec and Dan could not. They had behaved appropriately by growing up and leaving home—where the role of mother lived. Now I, too, had to leave that idea of home. I must find the way to live life whole-heartedly where I was now. Only if I committed fully to my own life would I be able to die feeling it had been complete. I had had glimpses of this truth before, but only now when I was feeling vulnerable to old age, sickness, and death, did I understand it with my heart.

I let go of old expectations and opened to how things actually were. I saw that looking to Alec and Dan to make me feel good about myself was the very thing that prevented me from self-acceptance. And I understood something about love I hadn't realized before. Perhaps love flows mostly one way, outward—from me to my sons, from them to their children. It doesn't return directly, as I had been wanting. It makes a big, wide circle to eventually come back through others.

The Shuso's Way Seeking Mind talk was the opportunity to step forward as I truly was, offering my life experience to others. I worried my topic would make me look like a bad mother, but the tradition is for the Shuso to offer the truth about her practice. I decided to do this as fully as I could. I had to give the talk twice, once to my home sangha, and once to our Vancouver, B.C. sister sangha where Norman was also the guiding teacher. The Vancouver talk came first at a weekend retreat there. As Shuso I was a retreat leader and had the honor of sitting up front with Norman, looking out at the students in zazen. There were at least sixty people in attendance, three times the number who would attend the Red Cedar sesshin. I realized I knew, at most, ten of these students. I had composed the talk thinking of my small, home sangha members as the audience. Here in Vancouver most of the students were strangers to me. How experienced were they in Zen? I wondered. How many might be brand new to Zen and not have any context into which they could put my confessional talk?

As the minutes passed in zazen, my alarm grew. I was to speak the next morning. Should I talk about something entirely different? What would be a better topic? Sitting in zazen but intensely focused on solving this unexpected problem, I frantically considered various topics, developing one or two in some detail. Finally, as the evening of zazen drew to a close, I realized that rewriting the talk at this point was impossible. I would have to give the talk I had prepared. A true Zen moment of facing the reality of the situation.

I was amazed and touched by the audience response. It seemed I had hit a chord about relationships between parents and adult children. Especially sweet were the thanks from several men who said they, too, had been estranged from their beloved adult children. Hearing how I had dealt with the problem was helpful to them. Because the talk was generously received, I discovered it was possible to be genuinely myself without fear of rejection.

Chapter Six

Autumn Light

At the end of my term as Shuso, a Zen friend asked me if the next step would be priest ordination. "Oh no," I reflexively replied. "I decided long ago that ordination was not for me." My thinking mind had not yet caught up with my recent emotional and spiritual growth. Being Shuso and doing psychological work on my relationships with Alec and Dan had liberated me from some long-held and restrictive views of myself. I could begin to see new possibilities. A few months later, at a weekend sesshin when I was in the role of Ino (zendo coordinator), I realized that there were no more reasons not to be ordained: My family was grown and gone; I was retired; and I wanted a worthwhile way to spend my remaining years. Maybe priesthood would not only be possible. It might be a terrific idea. I would have to stretch. I would have to keep studying and learning. I knew I would not be a perfect priest, but people would expect me to practice sincerely and to lead by example. I would have to be wholehearted. I felt I was ready. I decided to ask Tim if he would consider ordaining me. He had recently received priest *transmission* from Norman. This gave him authority to perform both lay and priest ordinations. Tim was receptive to my request but wanted advice from Norman and from his two priest colleagues in Vancouver, BC. I knew I was asking a lot of him so early in his authorization to ordain and supervise a new priest. Plus it was late in my life to be ordained. A priest is expected to assume significant duties in the sangha, but as I aged, my energy might wane, though it hadn't yet. I awaited the decision anxiously. A few weeks later, Tim told me that everyone agreed it would be all right for me to be ordained. We discussed the Buddhist works I should study. He said we would go forward slowly, to give our sangha time to get used to the idea. Then he told me I would also be required to take part in a three-month practice period at Tassajara, the Soto Zen monastery in California.

45

"I have to do *what?*" I gasped. Training at Tassajara was well known to be rigorous and demanding even for young people.

"A requirement for priest ordination," Tim repeated patiently, "is to do a three-month practice period at Tassajara."

I was horrified. I had no idea that time at Tassajara was required. "Surely I am too old. There must be something I could substitute? A community service project? Return to volunteering for Hospice?"

"No," Tim replied. "Tassajara is required. Think about it. We'll talk again next week."

During my forty-some years of practicing Zen, I had participated in countless seven-day residential sesshins. I lived at Sogenji in Japan for six weeks and did four additional residential sesshins there. In 2000 I did the three-week January practice period at Green Gulch. Much younger during those experiences, I managed the rigors of monastic life well. Now nearing my ninth decade, I feared three months at Tassajara would be too difficult.

Over the next week, I gave this bad news much thought, indeed. I had been to Tassajara years before for weeklong retreats. I knew the physical layout and terrain might not be easy for me to navigate. When Tim and I met again, I argued that because of my weak back I could not do the work expected of practice period students: "I can't carry heavy pots of food up from the kitchen to the zendo, so I can't be on a meal serving crew." I hated to play the disability card, a label I had always eschewed, but I was desperate. "I need much more sleep than the six hours maximum allowed by the monastery schedule," I added. "I'm simply too old to go to Tassajara,"

In point of fact, during the past two years I had begun to feel my age at our annual seven-day residential sesshin near Bellingham. Toward the end of the week I was physically so tired I could barely walk back to my cabin. I used to welcome the two-block walk across the retreat compound eight or ten times daily. It shook out the kinks from long hours of zazen. Now it exhausted me. And I worried that sleep deprivation at Tassajara might push me toward senile dementia. My sister, just six years older, suffered from dementia. This possibility held special resonance.

Tassajara is a beautiful place. During its summer guest season, people come at great expense from all over the world to attend retreats and workshops. I had stayed there three times and loved each experience. The exotic combination of sensual pleasure—delicious vegetarian food, dramatic narrow canyon setting, healing hot springs baths—and silent monastic life—robed monks, incense, and temple bells—make the Tassajara experience uniquely salubrious.

Practice period at Tassajara was another story. The monastery had been established by Suzuki Roshi in the 1960s as the first Soto Zen training monastery in the western world. It has lived up to its promise to train committed Zen students in the forms and practices of Buddhist ceremonies and teachings. Following the example of Japanese Zen monasteries, training at Tassajara has long had the reputation of being rigorous. From my earliest days as a Zen student I'd heard tales of its deprivations—unheated cabins in snowy winters, kerosene lanterns, ungodly wake-up times, long days of zazen. I was particularly intimidated by Tangaryo, the five-day "test" of the monks' sincerity to practice that precedes practice period. Even when I was thirty years younger, I was convinced I could never survive Tangaryo.

The rigor of practice period at Tassajara was not the only problem. I also hated not being able to pull my own weight. Doing what was asked without question, after all, was a Zen credo. I had always tried to fulfill this expectation, but Tassajara's monastery roles would require more strength and agility than I now had. At seventy-eight, I would already be unusual at Tassajara where most of the students would be thirty, forty, even fifty years younger. I dreaded being a special case, especially when it would mean others had to do my work on top of their own.

I recalled a seven-day sesshin at Green Gulch, when I was in my early fifties. I was assigned as a meal server for the week. On the first day, I injured my lower back carrying a heavy pot from the kitchen to the zendo and had to resign from the crew. The back spasm was so bad that I might have quit the entire sesshin. Wanting to prove my Zen chops, I stayed and sat through the pain the entire week. I focused on my back muscle spasm, following its bite as daily it moved slowly up my back. At each break after meals, I fled to my nearby room to lie down. On the final day, the spasm released through my left shoulder. A vivid experience of embodiment. Nearly thirty years older now, I knew I couldn't replicate that warrior-like determination.

What to do? Tim was following San Francisco Zen Center's protocol for priest ordination. His plan was for me to go to Tassajara immediately following ordination—before, as he joked, I grew even older. He appeared unwilling to yield. I must submit to the tradition of obedience to the lineage as represented by the teacher. Or forego ordination.

As I reflected deeply on what would be best for me, Tim sent me a wonderful talk, "On Being a Priest," by Norman. Here is a portion of that talk:

> Being a priest is a powerful archetype that you enter for better and worse. . . . Entering it you will become, whether you like it or not, a figure for healing in someone's life, in someone's psyche, in someone's heart, or you equally may well become a figure of confusion and upset in someone's psyche, in someone's life, for reasons that have nothing to do with who you are, what your personality is, or what your actions have been. This is possible. . . .
>
> To be a priest is to renounce—to let go of and give up. When you become a priest and you undertake that obligation, and you enter that archetype, it means to be a renunciant, to let go of everything you have, and to see every

person that you are and every thing that you have as only in the service of dharma. . . . that's a great freedom, or it's a great burden. . . .

[T]here are three practices of being a priest. The first practice is to be humble, to realize that we don't know so much, that our understanding of dharma is always limited, and that our experience only goes so far. And so we don't think, 'Oh, I'm a priest. I'm an expert. I know something.' We're just willing to do our best to share whatever small bit of the practice we've been able to absorb. We want to share it with others as they wish and as they need it. . . .

The second practice of priests is to see everyone as a Buddha, and to treat everybody that way. In the ordination ceremony it says, 'Now everyone is your teacher.' To see everyone as your teacher; to see everyone as sacred and special; everyone as important. . . .

The third practice is always trying to help others. Priests have this obligation. I find that in recent years I keep wanting to say this word in relation to priest practice: obligation. Priests have the obligation to help others. . . . And even if we can't do it very well, and I think a lot of us can't do it very well, we have to try. . . .

So that's the main thing: to be humble, to see everyone as Buddha, and always to try to help. That and putting on the okesa, protecting the okesa, and all that goes with that—chanting and bowing and offering incense. Putting on the okesa empowers you in that chanting and bowing in a special way, so that you can offer the benefit of that to others. . . . (Fischer 2008).

Norman's talk expressed the longing I had not myself been able to articulate about being ordained. I especially resonated with his insight that as a priest one can become a figure of healing in someone's life *or* a figure of confusion and harm without ever intending either. I had discovered that simply in being myself, for instance, taking up a space or role that someone else wants or resists, I can bring about suffering, despite my good intentions. My inability to rescue Dave had demonstrated this. I wanted to dive more deeply into both the profound sorrow and the amazing joy of being human. As a priest, I might better accept and be of help to others.

I knew Tassajara would be an enormous challenge. But Norman's beautiful words confirmed that it was the step I wanted to take. I would give it my all. I told Tim, "Okay. I'll do it." He would set things in motion, adding, "I will ask that you receive the accommodations you need for work assignments and getting enough sleep." I would enter the monastery as both a Zen elder and a brand new, novice priest. For practice period, I would be an ordinary monk. But for the first time in my Zen practice I would have a public role—an *archetype* as Norman had so beautifully described it—in the long tradition of Zen practice and structure. Was this archetype the wholehearted practice I longed for?

Tim and I set the date for *Shukke Tokudo* (priest ordination) on a Sunday in August the following year. Then I could go straight to Tassajara for the fall practice period. With advice and instructions from Zen sewing teacher Jean

Selkirk in Berkeley and material sent by San Francisco Zen Center sewing teacher, former Abbess Blanche Hartman, I began the powerful practice of sewing the okesa. Tim and Vancouver B.C. Zen sewing teacher Nin-en spent a full day with me, cutting out the material for the okesa. This entailed a complex metric measuring process that I never could have managed alone. I began sewing, following the idiosyncratic Japanese instructions of traditional okesa construction.

There were some thirty-five or forty pieces to sew together. I spent the next ten months, in the dim light of Northwest fall and winter days, sewing the okesa by hand with taupe colored thread on black cloth. I studied the complicated instructions for joining sections of the okesa—often counterintuitive, overlapping and inverted connections. Altogether there were twenty-one sections of three different lengths to be sewn together, then framed by a border in an equally complicated way.

Sewing the okesa is intended to be a meditation. The stitches are called *Namu Kie Butsu* stitches because as one sews, one chants, *"Na-mu, Ki-e, But-su"* (I take Refuge in Buddha) with each insertion, forward movement and pulling through of the needle. With this procedure I made innumerable stitches, each two millimeters in size and two millimeters apart, each one quavering and unique. When I grew distracted and forgot to say *Namu Kie Butzu* as I stitched, the stitches became uneven, and I had to backtrack and remove the poorly made ones. The chant steadied my hand and eye and poured all my attention into the okesa slowly coming into being in my hands. I made some large mistakes, such as not fully aligning one section of the okesa to its neighbor or discovering that one section had been cut too long for its place in the whole. Twice I had to take out hundreds of stitches. When I thought I could "get away with" letting a lesser error go, in the middle of the night or the next morning, I remembered I wanted to do the best work I could, so I removed the stitches and fixed the problem. A wonderful practice in devotion and patience.

As Tim had requested, I invited sangha members to participate in sewing by adding a few stitches. A few non-Zen friends, entranced by this tender practice of sewing the Buddha robe, also asked to add stitches. I sewed other ceremonial items—new *oryoki* cloths (for cleaning and wrapping the ceremonial, nested meal bowls), a new rakusu, a *zagu* (the rectangular cloth the priest puts on the floor to protect the okesa when bowing), and cloth envelopes for the okesa and rakusu. I had the *koromo* (formal robe) and *kimono* (undergarment) made by a professional, Mo Ferrell, in North Carolina, as those garments were beyond my sewing skills.

During the months of sewing, I asked myself why I was doing this—why was I becoming a priest? I remembered romanticizing ordination twenty years earlier. I no longer had those fantasies. Still, I had no words to answer the question. I just kept sewing. Then I recalled Norman's words about the priest's obligation to help others even if they don't do it very well. I knew how easy it was to be selfish, to feel afraid and separate from others. Perhaps I needed to be stretched beyond habitual limits, to be *required* to help. I did feel I was following my heart—perhaps at last my whole heart.

Ordination weekend arrived. My family members arrived from Florida for the events—Alec and his wife and their two teenaged daughters, Dan and his fiancée. I was overjoyed that they could come. I hoped their interest meant a closer relationship for all of us going forward.

On the Saturday afternoon the family and several sangha friends gathered in my back yard to conduct and witness my head shaving. After I lit incense and wrapped myself in a sheet to keep shorn hair off my clothes, Shudo, a Red Cedar priest, used her electric shaver to cut my hair down to a half-inch length. Then Dai-I, from Vancouver B.C. and also a priest, took over with shaving cream and a safety razor. Because my hair was very thick, she labored for over an hour, but at last I was completely bald except for a small tuft of hair that would be cut off during the ceremony. People took photos. Granddaughters gasped and giggled. I ran inside to inspect my appearance in the bathroom mirror. My head was not misshapen as I had feared it might be.

The sun now lower in the sky, I grew chilled without hair and embarrassed to still be the center of attention. We set out the picnic we had planned. After our meal, I passed out small thank you gifts to each participant. To Alec and Dan I gave broadside copies of a poem I had published ten years earlier about the generation gap I was then struggling with and described in my Way Seeking Mind talk as Shuso. They, themselves, now had growing and grown children. I thought the poem might resonate with them.

Both

The young crackle
with contempt
for the old.

The old combust
with indignation
at the young.

Having been both young and old,
I am well acquainted
with this wrathful symmetry.

Mirrors of each other's
deepest fears—
impotence, tyranny—

we mistake righteousness
for purity, fervor
for the proof of truth.

Co-evals in this ancient battle,
both must shed our serpent armor,
both must let our hearts be pierced. (Norton 2007)

Tokudo day started at the Dharma Hall with 6 a.m. zazen for sangha members, followed by a silent breakfast downstairs in the kitchen. At 10 a.m., keeping tradition, I went to the dokusan room to meditate by myself before the ceremony. I didn't sit down in zazen. Instead, I stood and gazed out the window at the meditation garden below. A sudden breeze on my newly shaved head startled me. I felt vaguely uneasy, as if on a precipice. The big moment was here, yet I couldn't identify what I was feeling. Was it hesitation? When I was sewing the okesa I had not been able to explain why I persisted so resolutely toward priesthood. I had just kept sewing. Now just before the ceremony, my body and spirit still seemed determined. I had to trust them.

I dressed for the ceremony. Over my white T-shirt and black slacks, I put on the white *juban*, the short-sleeved cotton blouse with a shawl collar that shows just above the neck folds of the black koromo robe. Next I put on the gray kimono made from soft batiste. Around my waist I wrapped a white three-inch wide elastic belt to hold the juban and kimono in place. Finally, I put on the white cotton *tabi* slippers required for Zen ceremonies. I had bought mine twenty years before in Japan. The tabis are constructed so that the big toe has its own "pocket" and the rest of the toes are enclosed together as in a mitten. My tabis were fastened by four, clever, little, flat hooks that fit the tabi tightly to the ankle. During the ceremony Tim would give me my black koromo with its long, Chinese style sleeves, and my sacred okesa.

Dressed in these traditional undergarments, rather like a bride about to enter her bed chamber, I was ready for my new incarnation. Now I felt some nervousness about how startling my shiny baldhead might be to waiting friends in the audience. I was glad the family, especially my granddaughters, had been present for the head shaving. My appearance now would not be so much for them to absorb. Having witnessed several priest ordinations, I knew what an amazing sight an ordainee makes on her/his entrance. I hoped I looked as beautiful as they had—at least spiritually. I couldn't help grinning at the spectacle I would be for my non-Zen friends.

At 11 a.m. when the ceremony was to begin, Nin-en came to get me. She had helped me cut out the material for the okesa, and she, along with Dai-I, had stayed at my house many times when they came down from Vancouver to sesshins at Red Cedar. We had become good dharma friends. I appreciated Nin-en'a calm and generous nature, so I had asked her to lead me into the ceremony. We hugged and then she walked ahead of me from the dokusan room in slow procession into the zendo. Surely, with my shiny, shaved head, elderly visage, and virginal clothing, I made a confounding vision. The zendo was full: twenty or so sangha friends, family members, and twenty to thirty friends from Bellingham and Seattle, all curious to witness the exotic transformation I would undergo. As happened when I was Shuso, I experienced the great joy of being warmly received.

The Tokudo ceremony was beautiful. Lots of chanting, exchanges between the doshi (officiating priest, Tim) and me as the various ceremonial items were sanctified and presented to me. The audience joined in some chants, making them part of the ritual. The ceremonial items were wrapped in white paper and tied with red ribbons. Tim held and passed each one three times over the incense bowl to bless it and then offer it to me. First was the black koromo, then the zagu, then the priest's black rakusu, then the okesa, and finally the oryoki set, a gift from the sangha. Except for the koromo and the wooden oryoki bowls, I had made all of these items. They were deeply familiar and precious to me. As I received the koromo and okesa, dharma friends helped me put them on. Nin-en helped with the koromo, and after Tim had ceremonially shaved the tuft of my hair, I was given my okesa. Dai-I and Myoshin, both priests from Vancouver B.C., helped me put it on— wonderful sisterly moments. Before the ceremony I think I had folded the okesa incorrectly, so there was some confusion and laughter before Dai-I and Myoshin rearranged it properly over my left shoulder.

During the ceremony, I was required to bow to Tim after receiving each item and putting on those that I was to wear. These were full bows to the floor, and I worried that I would step on my vestments when I kneeled. A friend in the audience told me afterwards that she was afraid I would get caught up in the voluminous robes. But somehow I managed to get up and down for each bow without stumbling or falling—moments of ceremonial grace.

Once I had donned the koromo but before I could receive the okesa, the Buddha Robe, Tim conducted the most curious part of this ancient ceremony, the ritual cutting of the tuft of hair left from the shaving the day before. This ceremonial shaving signifies the complete break with the novice priest's former life and her bodily commitment to the Buddhadharma. During this action, Tim chanted the following ceremonial verse three times:

The last hair is called the *shura*.
Only a Buddha can cut it off!
Now I will cut it off!
Do you allow me to cut it off?

And each time I replied:

Yes! I do!

Then Tim cut off the shura, and chanted:

Shaving your head and again shaving your head,

Cutting your attachments,

You are now on the path of the Buddha.

With the mind of complete enlightenment,

You will free all beings from suffering.

And I responded:

Freed from my ancient karma,

Freed from my worldly attachments,

Freed from form and color,

Everything is changed

Except my deep desire to live in truth with all beings.

The phrase, "freed from form and color" was particularly poignant because it reminded me of my lifelong pleasure, painting. For a moment I didn't want to relinquish the beauty of the world, though I knew that the meaning was to be freed not from beauty but from having a preference for it. Still, this was a tender moment of renunciation.

I turned to face the audience, and Tim offered his dharma talk to celebrate the occasion. I did not know what he would say and felt a mixture of curiosity and anxiety. He began by noting that I had considered being ordained for many years, since I was a student of Kobun Chino roshi forty years earlier. Tim continued:

> Our tradition is unusual in that our ordained people are not true monastics in the sense of living lives of poverty and celibacy under rule, and unlike other Buddhist orders we don't wear our robes all the time and we have a lot of flexibility about how we express our commitment. And yet it's that commitment which is as deep as any. As the ceremony says "from now enlightenment is your teacher, Buddha is your teacher, all beings are your teacher." We really mean this, we know we'll forget and that our confused self-centered attitudes will arise, but we are committed to remembering this. Norman suggests to us that the Zen priest has three main practices: be humble, see every person as Buddha, and try to help.. . .We also know that becoming a priest isn't gaining anything. It's the opposite, it's letting go of something. Letting go of our own agenda. Letting go of getting what we want. Letting go to some large extent of being comfortable. . . .You would have been happy enough to keep the name you received from your second jukai teacher, Tenshin Reb Anderson roshi, who gave you the name Zaren Shinge—Sitting Lotus, Deep Understanding— thirteen years ago in year 2000. And I think we might have done that, but I was thinking about the fact that you had another name before that, received from your first teacher, Kobun Chino Otogawa roshi, thirty-six years ago in 1977— Shunko Myoko—Spring Light, Wonderful Happiness. And I was thinking

about the many changes you've gone through in life and now at this point to be making yet one more big change. . . .

So I realized we should mark the power of your vow and the depth of this change by also changing your name one more time. Probably for the last time. So I picked a new name that includes one character from each of your previous Dharma names."Your new name is Shūkō Zakū—Autumn Light, Sitting in Emptiness. Kobun gave you Shunkō—Spring Light, all those years ago and it certainly seems like enough seasons have passed to change this first pair of characters to Shuko. Just one letter different in English, Spring Light passing naturally into Autumn Light, and autumn light is actually my very favorite quality of light all year. And what I appreciate about Autumn light somehow matches up with my appreciation for who you are. . . .

Tenshin gave you Zaren—Sitting Lotus, and for your second pair of characters I thought we'd keep his za—to sit—such a central part of our way. Learning how to just be in the middle of anything. And to za we add a little encouragement to continue your studies of the empty and boundless nature of all things with ku, the character used for emptiness shunyata. Which is also used for sky. So Zaku—sitting in emptiness. Or sitting in the sky if you like. To me this is a very important point, one I forget and remember again frequently. We have nothing solid to rest on. And our ability to feel into the utterly formless, fluid, changing nature of ourselves and others, and our world, to be able to feel that and be with it without being destabilized by it is probably the greatest gift that our way of practice has to offer the world. That is the root of true fearlessness. . . . (Burnett 2013).

I was surprised at this new name. Tim and I had agreed that I would keep the name Reb gave me, Zaren. For an instant I felt a stab of disappointment. But as I continued to listen to Tim's explanation, I was touched that he chose to honor my previous teachers and the names they gave me within this new name. I recalled that when I first became a Zen student, it was thought that one could have only one teacher. I felt very grateful to have had the support and guidance of several—Kobun, Reb, informally Norman, and now Tim as my ordination preceptor. I wholeheartedly accepted from now on I was *Shuko Zaku*, Autumn Light, Sitting in Emptiness.

Chapter Seven

Tassajara

A Zen legend exemplifies the sincerity needed for monastic practice:

A monk came to the monastery gate in wintertime and knocked to be let in. Inside, the gatekeeper called out, "What do you want?" "I wish to come in and practice here," the monk answered. "No, go away, you cannot come in." The monk stayed outside the monastery gate all night in the snow. The next morning he knocked again. Again the gatekeeper asked what he wanted, and the monk said he wanted to enter the monastery. The gatekeeper again told him to go away. The monk stayed all night in the snow, and in the morning, he knocked yet again at the monastery gate. The gatekeeper called out as before, "What do you want?" and the monk replied again, "I want to enter the monastery and practice here." The gatekeeper slowly opened the gate. The monk's sincerity had been demonstrated.

This cautionary tale came to mind as I embarked with fourteen other Zen students in two vans on the four-hour drive south from San Francisco Zen Center to Tassajara. The day was sunny with a light breeze—we would not be left out in the cold. When we drove through Carmel Valley's golden, rolling hills graced with grand, old live oak trees and spacious country estates, my mind drifted back to the times when I stayed at Tassajara during summer guest seasons. I recalled the dry, hot air (over 100 degrees F.), the scent of blooming flowers mingling with temple incense, scrub pine, sycamore, and madrone; the hushed, silty walkway through the monastery compound; the musical Tassajara Creek that defines one edge of the narrow valley. Despite my anxiety about practice period, I was pleased to return to this beautiful place.

As we dropped into the rugged mountains on Tassajara Road, the temperature rose noticeably, well into the 90s. Dust clouds from the rocky road swirled up around our van, obscuring our view as we lurched from one hairpin turn steeply down to the next. The deeper we descended, the more abruptly the canyon's rough walls loomed above us. Their sides were pitted with outcroppings of what appeared to be both granite and lava rock clinging to the mountainside. Bits of these rocky walls continuously crumble down to form the soft silt of the monastery walking path.

I knew these last fourteen miles of our journey would be challenging and take an hour to negotiate. Thirty years earlier, I had twice driven my car down this rugged road to attend summer retreats. On one trip, my brakes failed. I was going slowly and could nudge the car into the rocky upside of the road, scraping only the right fender, but it had scared me. This time the road was even worse. The van careened around to avoid the deep chuckholes or to climb out of them when they were unavoidable. Lurching downward, we van passengers were tossed around like loose luggage. Was the road objectively worse than it had been years before? Or was this discomfort due to my anxiety about going to Tassajara? Later I learned that Monterey County had not graded the road for the previous two years. Many weeks later when I was exhausted from practice period and ached to leave Tassajara, the thought of that road dissuaded me.

Finally we arrived at the monastery. It looked much the same as I remembered it. The large wooden zendo building was set uphill, overlooking the stone kitchen and dining room/dormitory buildings below. A courtyard gathering place stood between them. Individual wooden cabins, both old and newer, lined the gently sloping pathway in one direction, and the wooden and stone office building and guest rooms extended in the other direction. We would not see the newer Baths building and the Conference Center farther down the path until after our five-day Tangaryo initiation to practice period.

We disembarked from the vans, disoriented and wobbly after hours on the road. Several smiling resident monks rushed up to welcome us and help with our luggage. They showed us to our lodgings, escorted us to the dining room for lunch, and told us that we were to return there in thirty minutes for orientation and oryoki training, the ritual Japanese Zen form and equipment for eating meals in the zendo. I was billeted with seven other women in the dormitory above the dining room. Practice period students over age fifty-five were given rooms there because, unlike the cabins, the building could be heated. This was an amenity we older folks might appreciate as later in the fall temperatures dropped. The dorm was also just across the pathway from the zendo—a location I came to appreciate as I staggered toward zazen each morning at 4:10 a.m.

We each had a small, separate room (seventy to eighty square feet) with a raised futon cot, a tall venetian-blinded window, a small, un-curtained closet, and a small chest for our clothing. My room was spare and fairly clean. A shared bathroom was just down the hall. I had brought the bare minimum in

clothes and supplies plus my sleeping bag. I was surprised and a little envi-
ous when days later I discovered that some monks had set up fully furnished
bed-sit rooms: photos of partners and pets and Buddhist icons attractively
pinned on their walls, real bedding (sheets, blankets), nicely arranged toiletries on chests of drawers, and even small vases of flowers. It appeared that I,
by contrast, was on a three-month campout.

There was no time that first day for unpacking and settling into our
rooms. Instead we were off to our orientation to Tangaryo, which would
begin early the next day. Tangaryo is the traditional Soto Zen monastic
practice for testing the sincerity of the applicant's intention to enter the
monastery and practice intensively.

Tassajara has followed the Tangaryo tradition since the monastery was
established in 1967. Now we nineteen Tassajara initiates were about to
"knock on the monastery gate" and demonstrate our sincerity for five full
days of zazen. I suspect we all were afraid we might not make it through all
five days. I imagined if I didn't, I would be driven back up that terrible
Tassajara road and left at some bus stop, baggage in disarray, to await the
next bus north. I was determined to do my best to survive Tangaryo.

We gathered in the dimly lit dining room for orientation. Two men, in
whose charge we new monks would be for Tangaryo, instructed us. We
would not meet the Abbess, who was Head of the practice period, or any
other leaders, until we proved ourselves fit monks. The first was the *Tanto*, a
tall, middle-aged, senior priest who seemed he might, on occasion, be jovial.
He was responsible for the monks' training and smooth running of practice
period, including enforcement of all zendo rules and protocols. Interestingly,
in Japanese, *tanto* means "short sword or dagger." I would discover that as
disciplinarian, the Tanto had the final, firm word on what was permitted. The
second leader was the *Ino*, a serious looking, younger man, in charge of
coordinating activity in the zendo and leading the *doan-ryo*, the monks in the
zendo roles of chant leader, drummer, and bell ringer.

Still a little dazed from traveling, I found it hard to focus on the orientation information. But I understood the Tangaryo plan was for zazen in the
zendo from 4:20 a.m. to 9:00 p.m. for the next five days. We were instructed
as follows: We would have all our meals in the zendo, oryoki style. Following meals we would have a thirty-minute break to go to our rooms. Otherwise, we could leave the zendo only to go to the bathroom, using only the
three toilets situated immediately below the zendo. So that we could focus
entirely on zazen, we were not to go anywhere else for the duration of
Tangaryo. We were to observe strict silence, though in an emergency, we
were permitted to communicate with the Ino by writing a note and placing it
on his zabuton (mat).

I wasn't able to tell much about the other Tangaryo students. But I was
curious about them. There were slightly more women than men, several fifty-

five or older but only one man who looked as old as seventy. Everyone else seemed in their late twenties or thirties, as I had anticipated —almost as young as my two grandsons. I was clearly the oldest. The orientation ended with the reminder that we would not bathe or shower during the five days and nights of Tangaryo. This deprivation seemed to me, given the hot weather, even worse than five solid days of zazen. I never did learn the rationale behind this austerity—though I supposed that ancient monk banging at the gate didn't get a shower either.

Our orientation concluded, we were instructed to return to our rooms, dress in our robes, and go straight to the zendo. There we would have evening service followed by our first oryoki meal, a short break, and then the evening's zazen. Thus pushed headfirst into Tangaryo, I wondered if I would survive this baptism. It turned out that all of us, young and old alike, wondered this. Nevertheless, for the next five days we would "religiously" follow the Tangaryo schedule:

> *4:20 a.m.*—Wake up bell
> *4:50*—Zendo—zazen and *kinhin* (walking meditation)
> *6:20*—Morning service
> *6:55*—Breakfast. 30 minute break
> *7:25*—Self-directed zazen and kinhin
> *11:50*—Noon service
> *12:00*—Lunch. 30 minute break
> *1:30* –Self-directed zazen and kinhin
> *5:50*—Evening service
> *6:00*—Supper. 30 minute break
> *7:30*—zazen and kinhin
> *8:55*—Refuges chant
> *9:00 p.m.*—Bed

On the first day of Tangaryo, we awoke at 4:20 to the clanging wake-up bell rung by a monk running from one end of the monastery compound to the other. I leapt out of my sleeping bag, eager to be a monk at Tassajara. Riding the high energy of a new beginning, I hurried to the zendo with great purpose. Inside, I climbed up onto my assigned seat on the tan and plunged into zazen. On the left was a young man—twenty-six years old, the youngest practice period student—who sat absolutely still in perfect form: straight back, full lotus, relaxed and steady breath. On the right was a middle-aged German woman, twenty-five years an ordained priest but doing her first Tassajara practice period. Between these two exemplars was me, both the oldest monk and the newest priest. In the zendo silence, the only sound was the occasional, tiny click of the door being carefully opened and closed by the monks in charge.

As a newly minted priest I had a challenge the other Tangaryo monks didn't have: learning to put on my black okesa in the predawn dark using only the sense of touch. The okesa is donned in the zendo before the morning chanting and bowing service, using prescribed, complicated, and non-intuitive movements. Adding to its difficulty was having to do it while kneeling at one's seat, rather than standing up, which allows the material to fall easily from one's shoulders down to one's lower legs, before wrapping oneself in it. Throughout Tangaryo and much of the first month of practice period, this ceremonial dressing found me flailing about as if a tent had collapsed on me. Daily practice alone eventually helped me master this precious ritual.

In preparing for Tassajara, I had been especially anxious about Tangaryo because "word on the street" was that it required continuous zazen for five days, fourteen hours a day. I knew this would be too much for my back. At sesshins, I always started out on my cushion and sat there for as many days as I could before I gave in to back pain and repaired to a chair. However, in sesshins our bodies got frequent relief because we walked in kinhin between zazen periods and bowed during services. How would I survive Tangaryo? After much worry, I conceived a new strategy: From day one, I would vary my zazen positions frequently. I would alternate between sitting cross-legged, kneeling, sitting in a chair, and lying down on my back on a zabuton.

To ask permission to do this, before leaving for Tassajara I phoned the Tanto to propose this plan. He okayed it—signaling my good fortune to be at Tassajara in the 21st century. Twenty or thirty years earlier, supine zazen was out of the question. Even sitting in a chair was allowed by only a few Zen teachers. In those days, American Zen hewed closely to the Japanese practice of the full lotus, though if one's Western body couldn't manage it, the half lotus would be tolerated.

As it turned out, because no bells were rung during Tangaryo to begin and end periods of zazen, everyone could change positions at any time throughout the day. All that was required was that we move quietly and not disturb others. This unexpected provision greatly eased my passage through Tangaryo.

The late September air was hot and very dry. I soon found I became so parched that I had no saliva even to swallow. We were not permitted to have water bottles in the zendo, so we all discovered a defensible reason for getting up from zazen: For our health we must go outside to drink from the water bottles we stored on the shoe shelving on the *engawa* (the zendo's surrounding porch).

Day two of Tangaryo was challenging. Though I had slept well, I was drowsy the entire morning (seven grueling hours, all before lunch). It was cold that day and because my head was shaved, I lost body heat continuously. Finally, convinced that being chilled constituted an emergency, I wrote a note to the Ino, asking permission to wear a hat, normally not allowed in the zendo. Not hearing anything from him for several hours, I decided that his silence was a Yes. From that afternoon onward until my hair grew out sufficiently, when it was chilly I wore a wool knit hat.

Next, it was time that was the problem. It moved so slowly. I hadn't realized my mind moved much faster than time did. On a break outside to drink water, when I checked the clock there, I found I had been sitting for only thirty minutes. I had thought two hours had passed. That day I squirmed and sighed and changed sitting positions at least eight times in each of the four-hour segments of the morning and afternoon sessions. This was the bedrock Buddhist practice of No Preferences, accepting whatever is in the moment. I had endured similar discomfort before in sesshins. I must simply apply patience and effort. Time and the changes that never failed to occur as it passed would get me through. I had been told that Tassajara would be my training as a priest, but Tangaryo seemed more a test of my qualifications to be a Zen practitioner. Student or priest, there was no difference, though if I failed Tangaryo, I might not be allowed to continue as a priest. I bore down.

That afternoon, still struggling with physical and mental discomfort, I tried to placate my agitated mind with various traditional techniques. I prayed to the Buddhas and Bodhisattvas to "shine their light on me," as Tim had suggested when he wished me good luck at Tassajara. I focused on the tiny click of the door latch as occasionally a student left or entered the zendo; the twisting sound when outside the zendo a monk opened a water bottle to drink and then set it back on the shelf with a soft bump; muted footsteps down the wood and dirt steps to the bathrooms; more distant, soft foot falls on the sandy path as a resident monk passed by quietly, respectful of our silence; the occasional distant clunk of a pan or pot and a muffled voice from the kitchen down across the way; the whispery rub of a monk rearranging her robes as she changed positions on her zafu; an occasional deep inhale and sigh of a fellow sufferer. I was not alone in this deep venture.

There was much to appeal to my other senses: the fragrant scent of sandalwood incense early in the morning as it wafted from the altar; the soft flickering light of altar candles; the changing daylight through the zendo's parchment screen windows as the earth turned from dawn to noon to dusk and inky night. The shadowy, still forms of the other monks, all in black.

The most energizing and welcome of sensations came at meal times: the muted footsteps of the approaching meal servers—four or five monks carrying pots of food up from the kitchen to serve us as we sat on our cushions; the varied smells and tastes of the simple but delicious food for our oryoki bowls: nutty grains for the Buddha bowl, the first and largest bowl holding about a cup of food; a rich broth or steaming scrambled eggs or a green vegetable for the middle bowl, holding about a half cup; and about a quarter cup for the third bowl of fresh fruit or salad greens or almonds or yogurt. The servers, themselves, were a treat to watch as they moved swiftly around the zendo stopping and bowing before serving us in pairs. We signaled the amount of food we wanted for each bowl by lifting our right hand when the server had given us enough. The energy and precision with which the servers moved fascinated me, so graceful and efficient in their choreography.

Appreciating these sensory pleasures, I was reminded that in daily life, I forget to note such delights because I am usually thinking about other things. Even in zazen my mind often dwells on aches and pains, emotional ups and downs, or habitual anxieties and preoccupations. But the practice of noticing all that is available in just the present moment is central to Zen practice. I appreciated that this unstructured Tangaryo zazen invited one into the present in all its richness. What better was there to do but to be alive in the flow of time?

Thus Day Two passed, my mind and body going in and out of sensation, discomfort, misery, and delight. Toward late afternoon I began to have spontaneous visual hallucinations that arose on the wall I faced just two feet in front of me. The wall was white adobe supported every three or four feet by vertical, five-inch-wide, reddish-brown studs of coarsely grained wood. As I gazed softly at the wall, the wood grain lines began to waver and flow in various beautiful patterns. I had experienced such visual distortions, termed *makyo,* during sesshins before and knew they were not indicative of any spiritual attainment. However, each time these makyo bloomed, as it were, I enjoyed their arising and falling before I shook myself mentally back to viewing the simple wall. Though uninvited, makyo helped pass the long Tangaryo hours. On the final two days of Tangaryo I also hallucinated handwriting on the wall. It was much like a handwritten letter in which the lines tilt upward as they go down the page. I couldn't read what the writing said, but I appreciated the irony of the message: The handwriting was, indeed, on the wall.

On Day Three of Tangaryo, in the early afternoon suddenly the silence of the zendo was obliterated by a terrific roar from some kind of motor just outside and below us. It was deafening and continuous. What on earth could it be and why was it permitted during Tangaryo? As time went on—it continued for most of the afternoon—I realized that it was some sort of truck vacuum, though I didn't know its purpose. I was annoyed (I later heard that some Tangaryo monks were very upset by the disruption), but there was nothing for it but to accept and reside within it, unpleasant as it was. Some days later I learned that this was the annual cleaning of the monastery septic tanks. Was it traditionally scheduled for Tangaryo week for our amusement or as another test of our sincerity?

That evening was capped by a rodent that suddenly ran over my bare foot as I sat in zazen. I gasped, jerked up, and shrank away, drawing my robes close. The young monk on my left did the same, agreeing in a whispered, "Mouse!" I never saw it. I just felt its tiny feet. I learned later it probably was a rat. This was an occasion to speak to the Ino at the end of the evening. I did so in a whisper. Clearly annoyed at my breaking silence, the Ino assured me he knew about the rodent and was taking steps to deal with it. I was abashed but gratified when the next night, it sounded like a monk had been posted out on the engawa during evening zazen to chase away further rodent visitors. Dealing with pests such as this was a real challenge in Buddhist practice, the first precept of which is No Killing. I didn't envy the Ino's responsibility.

On Day Four, after repeatedly falling asleep on my zafu all morning long, I felt discouraged. What was I doing here? What was I trying to prove? I lay down on the zabuton for zazen. As I gazed up at the pine paneled ceiling, the knots and wood grain slowly formed a face of a sad, old man. The face looked down sorrowfully and whispered sympathetically, "Many of our lives are like yours." I didn't know what to make of this statement, but it seemed to mean that we all suffer and feel our situation is too much for us. Then he said, "Seek joy in others. Take joy in their being." With these words, part of his face turned into that of a joyful child. Gazing up at this old man-child, I vowed to seek happiness at Tassajara by being a part of the sangha. I knew this vision was just another makyo, but that did not diminish its diverting and salutary effect. I would try to make friends here.

Finally Day Five arrived—the last of Tangaryo. I awoke at 4:10 a.m., *before* the wake-up bell, with renewed determination. The day would prove to be hot again. The morning was hard. I was sleepy, bored. The mind couldn't focus on the breath or any sounds, as it had before. This was the dreaded hindrance of *torpor.* At mid-morning, apparently to distract and amuse us, two resident monks came in and noisily cleaned the zendo, moving behind and around us, slamming zabutons and zafus with great thumpings on the floor to drive out dust.

Later, during the long afternoon zazen, I was unable to direct my mind to meditation practices as I had done earlier. Taking a cue from the joking cleaners, I succumbed to amusing myself. A song came to mind, but I couldn't remember its title. It was from a 1950s movie, "Picnic," but what was the name of the song? I remembered the actors and how they danced so romantically to the song, but what were their names? I recalled scenes from the movie; I felt the mood of the romance between the man and woman. Gradually over the next hour or so their names drifted up from my unconscious, first William Holden, the male lead, then Kim. . . Somebody. After more time: Kim Novak. But what was the song title? I could hear the orchestra playing it, but the title eluded me. Finally it appeared: "Moonglow!" I felt guilty that I had amused myself for at least one entire period of zazen. Nonetheless I was grateful to know that if I was patient and attentive, I could count on my mind to recall what I sought. A pretty nice lesson about the mind, one of many mind features I would discover at Tassajara.

Late afternoon on the fifth day of Tangaryo, after the evening service and oryoki dinner, the Tanto dismissed us to go to the Baths. At last! Though I had stopped waiting—had accepted zazen in perpetuity—I was delighted to be released. Five days without a bath, now we could shower, soak in the mineral water plunges, and break the silence we had kept since entering Tassajara. We laughed with relief and pleasure as we left the zendo, collected our shoes and our water bottles from the engawa shelves, and went to our rooms to take off our robes, grab a towel and head down the path to the Baths. My dorm mates and I hugged. We congratulated each other on having made it through Tangaryo. Along the pathway to the Baths, I exchanged happy greetings with other monks:

"Wow! Wasn't that amazing?" "Yeah, I didn't think I could do it, but we all did it!"

"Yes. I've never experienced such radical quiet! It was beautiful!"

"Me either. It was wonderful. Really, a lot easier than I thought it would be, too!"

Full of energy and gratitude, we almost danced to the Bath House. In the women's shower, each of us lavished liquid soap and shampoo on our bodies and bald heads. After having had only cold water splashes for five days at our bathroom sinks, we luxuriated in the steaming hot water. Rinsing off in the shower, one by one we entered the hot springs plunge, a lovely blue-tiled pool about five feet deep and ten by ten feet square, set inside ceiling-high glass doors that looked out on a wooden deck and riparian garden along Tassajara Creek.

As each of us sank into the 108 degree F. bath, we moaned with animal pleasure and settled onto one of the tiled ledges to sit or lie down and soak. From the discipline of Tangaryo to this delicious reward for the body. What a contrast. We didn't talk much. Though we had spent the last five long days together, we didn't know each other in any social way. Partly from shyness and partly from the sheer pleasure of the Bath, we continued in silence. Our common experience—and gratitude—was deeper than words.

At 7:00 p.m., we were back in our robes and in the zendo to be instructed in our role in the ceremony we would take part in the next morning at 5:30 a.m. to open the practice period. In my post-Bath sybaritic state, I found the instructions hard to follow. I recalled the confusion I had experienced on arrival six days earlier. At least this mental state was familiar. I hoped my companions had grasped the instructions better than I had. I would follow their lead the next morning when forty residential monks and priests would join us in practice for three months.

Chapter Eight

Learning the Ropes

Tangaryo completed, we students were welcomed by the Tassajara residents as practice period monks and assigned new seats in the zendo. Mine was on the opposite side from where I sat during Tangaryo. Now I was between two women. One was a small, slender, and composed young woman with long auburn hair, who did not make eye contact with me (then or ever). The other was a forty-ish woman with shaved head and okesa, who sat energetically, emanating fierce determination. Together we cast off to ride out the storms and doldrums of practice period. The Regular Schedule was similar to the Tangaryo schedule, only more rigorous. Each day began an hour earlier and had regimented periods of zazen signaled by bells, services, bows, and chants.

The candlelit zendo was quite dark mornings and evenings and in twilight the rest of the day. The dimness and silence established a comforting blanket of assurance that all was as it should be. We monks were where we were meant to be. Bells marked the periods of zazen and kinhin. Zendo leaders modeled the correct forms for how to hold our hands, walk, bow, approach, and get up on our cushions; prepare oryoki bowls for meals; and afterward clean them. And finally, how to leave our seats and exit together in two comingling lines.

Each morning we settled onto our zafus by 4:20 a.m. Flickering candles illuminated the large altar Buddha in the zendo center and cast our monks' shadows softly on the walls. The serenity of the space inspired devoted sitting. In the dark of early morning zazen, the only sounds in the zendo came from the back door being quietly opened and closed:

"Click—snuff—clack" as a monk carefully opened the door, softly stepped barefoot out onto the engawa, then gently pulled the door closed. Several minutes of deep, shimmering silence followed. Then these tiny sounds again softly punctuated the quiet—"Clack—snuff—click" as a monk re-entered the zendo. During the first hour of zazen these small sounds quietly urged me to wake up, wake up.

The effort made not to disturb anyone or anything exemplified the focused attention of monastic training. Throughout practice period, the leaders instructed us to pay close attention every moment to what we were doing and to do only what was necessary, no more, no less. In this way we could live fully in the present moment, where, as the Buddha taught, we can be free from suffering. Sitting in the Tassajara zendo, with its fifty-year legacy of the finest American and Japanese Zen teachers and students, was inspiring. It was also a respite from the urgent schedule of tasks and trainings into which we monks were pressed daily.

In my regular life after retirement thirteen years earlier, I took two leisurely hours to prepare for the day. Now mornings started at 3:40 a.m. and allowed only twenty minutes to get ready. At the clamor of the wake-up bell, as if rushing to a fire, I vaulted from bed in the pitch dark, fumbled for the lamp light on the bedside chest, dashed to the bathroom for the morning's ablutions, my shaved head a time-saver. Back in my room, I pulled on underwear, shirt, pants, and threw down my yoga mat onto the tiny floor space, and quickly lay down to do five minutes of hip opener exercises and spinal stretches. These morning stretches were essential to being able to stand upright and walk without stiffness and pain. Next I straightened out my sleeping bag and pillow, put on my juban, kimono, and koromo, and gathered up my okesa in its envelope. Grabbed a flashlight, shut the room door behind me, and exited onto the still dark dorm porch. Found and scuffled into my clogs and headed down the dorm steps for the zendo across the path and up the four broad, gradually inclining stairs. Left clogs on the shoe shelf and took a deep breath to compose myself after the intense rush to be on time.

We monks entered the zendo singly, carrying our folded okesa or rakusu in its envelope in both hands at eye level. We walked past the main altar, made a *gassho* (brief standing bow) to the Tanto, who was seated where he could observe each monk's entrance and posture. It hurt my lower back to walk and carry something at eye level, so I worried that I never passed muster. I scooted by the Tanto with as much dignity as I could summon and arrived with relief at my seat. This daily mad dash from a dead sleep to sitting composed on my zafu was quite a shock to my old body, but I performed it with determination every day for all three months of practice period.

That first day I focused on the instructions the Ino gave us earlier about comportment in the zendo: When we entered in the morning, we were to use the front door. If we left individually to go to dokusan or an assignment, we used the back door. When we left as a group, such as after meals and at day's end, we used the front door. If we were late arriving, we must enter through the back door, do three full bows, and then go as silently as possible to our seat. Fearing I would surely screw that up, I contrived never to be late the whole three months, adding to my daily morning stress.

At our seats, of course, we were to sit silently facing the wall and not change position during the thirty-minute zazen periods. In the morning, after the first period there was a five-minute interval in which we could change positions if needed before the bell was rung three times to signal the second period of zazen. Between all other periods of zazen, we rose from our cushions to do ten minutes of kinhin, the slow, composed walk in single file around the half of the zendo where we were seated. Kinhin is a meditation on breath and movement. On the inhale, the monk lifts and places her foot a few inches forward of her standing foot and begins picking up her other foot. On the exhale, she slowly places the raised foot on the floor. This practice aligns and refreshes the mind/body. I was accustomed to the protocols for zazen and kinhin, but I did need to learn the walking pattern for kinhin in this zendo.

The preparations for the daily morning service were more complex than those in my home sangha. We had to rise from the tan, pick up our zabutons and zafus, and place them, two by two, on the floor, facing the altar. There we stood and did nine full bows and then sat to chant the sutras. At various additional times during the service we stood again and bowed onto our zabutons. Before the chanting, a monk at each end of the zendo collected chant books from a bookcase and distributed them to the monks on her side of the room. Because my seat was at the back, I often had this task. Usually I couldn't move quickly enough to distribute the books before the chanting began. Knowing my slowness was annoying, I was reminded daily that my age impeded success at Tassajara.

When we left the zendo for a break or at the end of the day, we followed a graceful, choreographed walking pattern. The four practice period leaders led the departure, by first circling their side of the zendo and then exiting through the front door. Then the monks from the far corners of both sides led unfurling lines of monks swiftly toward the altar. As we passed the altar the two lines intermingled into one line to exit the front door. We were never given any instruction on the particulars of this or other zendo forms. We were expected to master them through observation. This was a challenge for me, ever anxious about making mistakes and always wishing for more information than we were given. Fortunately, the basic forms for moving and bowing and standing were familiar from many years of practice. Quite soon I felt comfortable, despite my initial ignorance of the nuances peculiar to Tassajara. I enjoyed the silence and evident concentration of the monks around me, most of whom were long-term residents, not fellow Tangaryo initiates.

Early on, as part of this daily attention to every detail, I vowed to take good care of my body: I would eat moderately and healthily, as would be possible with our oryoki diet—lots of grains, fruits and vegetables, few to no sweets. Avoid caffeine as it would make it harder to nap during the day or sleep at night. Exercise daily, doing yoga or swimming, as well as walking up and down the length of the monastery compound. Nap every day. So I could absorb and appreciate my experience, take a few minutes every day to reflect and write about it. Take advantage of the rich experience of the four practice leaders by regularly requesting dokusan and private interviews. In these I could bring questions and observations about the mental states I was experiencing. In my practice notebook I would keep a copy of each of the schedules—regular day, work day, personal day, and sesshin—so I would always know where I was supposed to be and when. I would pour all my determination, energy, and self-management skills into succeeding as a Tassajara monk.

I had many unanswered questions those first weeks of practice period about the way Tassajara functioned. When and why did we occasionally eat a meal in the dining room rather than in the zendo with our oryoki bowls? Where was the laundry area and when was there time to wash our clothes? By hand? I was surprised to learn there were no washing machines. Where was the library and what was our study assignment? What time did study period start and end? How long was *soji* (temple cleaning), which directly followed Study Hall? When and where were we priests supposed to wear our okesas and when and where not? When it was cold could we wear hats in the zendo? What about socks? Where was the *Tenken* (time keeper) sign-out sheet located and what information was required on it? When would we receive instructions about our jobs? We were never given an orientation to these details. The schedule was too tight to allow time to ask questions, let alone to know whom to ask.

I studied the day's schedule posted on the dining room door. I copied it into a small notebook where I kept notes on all our protocols and on what I learned from the dharma talks the leaders gave. I obsessed about being on time and in the right clothing for each event. The Ino's stern admonitions reverberated in my mind: "You are to be on your cushion at the start of the third roll-down of the *Han.*" The Han was the heavy wooden slab hanging outside the zendo and struck in a three-part cadence to call us to the zazen. And "Everyone is expected to sit the final period of zazen in the evening." Oh, I could never go to bed early, though I knew I would often long to.

Most of us new monks struggled the entire first month to learn the specifics of each day's schedule and to carry them out correctly. The biggest challenge for everyone may have been a subtle one: Our schedule replicated the Japanese monastic tradition of giving the monks a partial day off on days having the numbers five and nine in their dates. This created a five-day weekly rotation of four days of community activity and one partial day off for personal time. After a lifetime of seven-day weeks, five days may have been unconsciously disorienting. Eventually we lost track of what conventional weekday it was. Except for needing to contact someone in the outside world (which I rarely did), knowing which calendar day it was became irrelevant. We monks learned to communicate with each other about time solely in terms of which kind of day it was, Regular, Work, Personal, or Sesshin. Once my brain fully adapted to this cycle, my daily dizziness subsided.

On top of this subtle adjustment in our biorhythms, we often had to adjust to smaller schedule variations. Sometimes the leadership added or subtracted a Regular day in order to schedule the correct number of Sesshin days. Or at the last minute they changed a dharma talk or ceremony, which would have occurred in the zendo, to a presentation in the dining room. These changes usually were not announced except on the monks' assignment chart outside the zendo. I was not on a regular work crew, such as for meal serving, so I was not even aware of this communications mechanism until the third month of practice period. This explained my repeated surprise (and annoyance) at the frequent, unannounced schedule changes. On paper these adjustments seem like very minor perturbations, simple enough to absorb. However, until I was well "broken in," I experienced them almost as body blows. No doubt old age played a role in this strong reaction.

As time went on, the body would become more and more the singular locus of my Tassajara experience. Having to learn so many new behaviors at once with so little information was particularly difficult. I had always prided myself on my energy and adaptability, but for the first time, being "stuck in my ways" seemed to apply. Before Tassajara, I had had control over daily life. I could modify or even avoid activities that were too quick or complex or difficult. Now I was immersed with much younger people for whom the pace and complexity could be challenging but probably not overly stressful as it was for me. I was in good physical shape. I was experienced in Zen practice. I had a fighting chance at conquering the schedule, but this first month was harrowing. And because practice period continued apace for two more months, I never got ahead of its exhausting impact as the younger monks seemed to do.

The altitude of Tassajara (1,637 ft.), the hot weather, and the extreme aridity of the climate (California was in a severe drought) were other factors in the difficulty I had adapting to monastery life. Back home in Washington, I lived at sea level in a marine climate with plentiful rain. Tassajara's climate was a shock to my body.

Part of the adjustment problem was of my own making, of course. I arrived at Tassajara assuming that as a priest I must take part in all practice period activities and do them perfectly. This was not only an impossible goal, it was also an unnecessary one—one that confused me about both the training offered and my role with respect to it. To deal with the pressure I believed was on me, however, right off I set about figuring out how to adjust my body to the schedule, rather than how to adjust the schedule, which in regular life I might have done. I needed some daily naptime to make up for the insufficient hours of sleep at night. I had to identify the times in the schedule when my absence would be least critical to the monastic mission of wholehearted practice. I learned that dharma talks and services were mandatory, so I needed to work naps around those. Also, I had to figure out when in the day a nap would be most beneficial. When would I be most tired and would fall asleep most readily? What physical symptoms signaled that an immediate nap was essential? The calculus of when to nap became my highest priority, a daily imperative to solve.

Despite determined planning, initially my fatigue did not let up. My legs were heavy and my lower back ached. Often I was almost unable to drag myself up the gently ascending steps to the zendo. Sometimes I couldn't get enough oxygen. My mind was dull, confused, anxious. I noticed I was usually most tired after *soji* (temple cleaning), six hours into the morning. I decided this was when I should take a daily nap. The problem was that this was also when dharma talks occurred—once a week during the regular schedule, daily during sesshins. So when I heard that a talk would be given, I skipped the nap and struggled to stay awake even though the talks invariably were interesting and helpful.

Some nights, despite my fatigue—or perhaps because of it—I didn't sleep well and was extra tired in zazen the next morning. I nodded off repeatedly, jerking awake just before falling off my cushion. I hated the heavy dizziness in my head and stomach as sleep repeatedly overtook me. I knew sleepiness during zazen could be a sign of mental resistance. Was I resisting the program? Certainly I was frustrated by the persistent dearth of information and confusing schedule changes. If I understood better what was happening, I might relax more. I might sleep at night rather than in zazen. Or perhaps eventually I would just tire of wanting to understand what was happening. Meanwhile I had to put up with my confusion and sense of failure.

For priests, the tight monastery schedule created an additional challenge. All monks had to change clothes for different activities throughout the day and usually had no more than ten minutes to do so. For monks who were not ordained, this change was relatively simple. They put on or took off their black robe and possibly a belt. For priests, the clothing change was more elaborate. We changed two to four garments: juban, kimono, koromo, and okesa. For work practice, we changed out of our robes entirely and put on work clothes. For bathroom visits we removed both our okesa and koromo as they are considered sacred. For study hall and talks given outside the zendo, we removed our okesa and wore our rakusu. For the first several weeks of practice period, learning what to wear and when added significantly to the stress I experienced. I had been ordained only two months earlier, so I was also still learning how to put on, take off, and fold my okesa correctly. During one or two of the daily interstices between events, it was impossible to use the bathroom. There simply wasn't enough time to disrobe and re-robe and still be on time for the next activity. Strategies for getting to the bathroom became a necessary preoccupation until my body accommodated the schedule rather than the other way around.

I gradually accommodated myself to monastery life that first month, but I was perplexed about when the priest training I was sent to receive would begin. We were not studying any texts, as I had expected. Our focus seemed to be entirely on following the schedule and learning the many practice forms. The protocols were exacting and almost all physical—how to stand, walk, sit, bow, hold our hands, hold our bowls in the zendo. Every aspect of correct behavior required continuous mindfulness even to approximate. It took all my concentration and effort to be physically where I was supposed to be and do what I was supposed to do. I found no time or mental space to reflect on the meaning of all these activities. I had to give all my effort just to doing them.

What I didn't realize until long after I had returned home from Tassajara was that I had been kindly exempted from several major roles required of the other Tangaryo monks. Before coming to Tassajara, I had negotiated exemption from serving meals due to my weak back. Once there, I was also excused from a second demanding assignment: *Jikido*, a rigorous role through which Tangaryo monks rotated every fourteen or fifteen days. Jikido was similar to the ceremonial role I had had when cook's assistant at Sogenji in Japan twenty years earlier, but it involved much more than opening and closing the monastery.

In this twenty-four hour responsibility, the Jikido cleaned the entire zendo single handedly during the daily three-hour work period—sweeping, brushing, dusting, and putting in order each of the sixty zabutons and zafus. After dinner, she lit kerosene lamps outdoors at specific points along the monastery walkways. After dark, she put the day's food waste in compost buckets and put away sweeteners in the outdoor coffee area. That night she slept alone in the zendo to protect it from invaders. (This was similar to what I did to close Sogenji's grounds, shouting an incantation to scare away evil spirits.) Next morning she rose at 3:30 a.m. to help open the monastery for morning zazen. She hit a han located near the more remote cabins so those monks could hear when to go to the zendo, and snuffed out the kerosene lamps lit the previous evening. During the daytime the Jikido had various other tasks, such as ringing bells to announce activities. I was only dimly aware of the nuances that comprised this important role because I did not have to do it. But I knew each of the responsibilities had to be executed at very specific times in exactly correct ways. Plus many Jikido tasks occurred in the dark, when I might have stumbled and injured myself, running to keep on schedule as was necessary.

Jikido was so far beyond my physical capabilities at age seventy-eight that I didn't realize at the time how grateful I should have been to be excused from it. I was just relieved I didn't have to do it. I was so engaged in keeping up with the schedule that I couldn't see that Jikido training was the norm if I had been up to doing it. Blind to this fact, well into practice period I was still wondering why we did not have a specific course of study. Finally, I asked the Abbess when we would be assigned a Buddhist text. Her reply surprised me: "We have our daily study period in the morning, and the work and practice assignments are also part of the training." Finally I began to see that our daily routines *were* our training—in mindfulness, mental acuity, fealty to the traditional forms, and even physical fitness in order to perform the roles and ceremonies properly. Training had been occurring from the first week. What better example of how our individual experience and expectations define our reality?

A final example of training I did not receive was for the role of *doshi*. This is the priest's role during services. Tangaryo students who were also priests—there were three of us—were trained to lead the evening service and required to perform the role at least twice during practice period. I was exempted from this because the monastery rule was that to be doshi, one had to have been a priest for at least six months. I had been ordained only two months earlier, so I was not eligible. Again I was relieved to be exempted from this exacting role, which later I would learn in my home sangha, under much less performance pressure.

I wasn't up to all the training the younger Tangaryo monks received, but just following the daily changing schedule had a beneficial impact. The shorter "week" rotation through four types of days helped break down my habitual reliance on planning ahead and trying to understand everything cognitively. I began living more in the moment. Some of my unconscious conditioning rose to the surface where I could begin to work with it.

When gradually and eventually I realized how things worked and what was expected at Tassajara, I began to observe and appreciate the other monks in their practice roles. I noticed that the three or four monks who shared the Tenken role had the unenviable job of checking attendance each period of zazen to see who, if anyone, was missing from the zendo. When a missing monk had not signed out on the "Tenken sheet," the Tenken had to go find him. I thought this "policing" role might be difficult. I imagined the Tenkens struggled not to feel annoyance with monks who didn't follow the rules. I bet they had to work hard to cultivate patience and generosity as they carried out their guardian duties. The monastery experience I had in Japan twenty years earlier taught me that this close supervision, so draconian to American eyes, arose from the monastic commitment to be responsible for each and every monk's safety. At Sogenji, which was located in a large city, we monks could leave the monastery on a Personal Day to run errands, take a walk or, in my case, go swimming. But first, we had to ask permission of the Abbot himself. And on our return we had to tell him that we were safely back. I found this requirement difficult because my Japanese was so poor. I always stumbled through the words I was supposed to say. Asking for permission also made me feel like a child. But this was an important monastery ritual, which I learned to follow faithfully.

A month or so into practice period at Tassajara, I also realized that the Doan-ryo monks practiced their roles nearly every day for several hours. These monks "played" the drums and bells, led the chants, and kept time for zazen. It was an honor to be in the Doan-ryo and a big responsibility. Those six monks, led by the Ino, met in the zendo every work period to discuss and practice their roles. They also learned and practiced the frequent special ceremonies. Their mission was to perform and coordinate the zendo instruments. They worked tirelessly to make our services and ceremonies beautiful and meaningful. Their devotion and hard work were an inspiration, and apparently their roles were rewarding. I overheard one young Doan-ryo monk remark that having this role had, for the first time, made him fully appreciate the value and power of Zen practice. His statement reminded me of the importance of whole-hearted practice. I felt a rush of gratitude for the Doan-ryo's example and service to us all.

Chapter Nine

Full Immersion

In the first week of practice period, the Abbess appeared in our midst and deftly began to frame the teachings she and the other practice period leaders would offer us. First they focused us on working with our individual minds in practice. Later they would guide us in practicing in community.

A tall, slim woman in her late fifties, the Abbess was one of twelve abbots to lead San Francisco Zen Center since it was founded in 1962, only three of them women. There are many Zen women priests in the Western world today, some filling leadership roles in large Zen centers, some heading small Zen sanghas. Only a handful has risen to the level of abbot. The Abbess's graceful comportment in the zendo that morning reflected this high honor. The color of her robes distinguished her office from that of the other senior priests, who wore traditional black robes and brown okesas. The Abbess's impeccable koromo was a soft gray, her okesa, taupe. Both colors complemented her rosy complexion and elegant, shaved head.

Before delivering her dharma talk, the Abbess conducted the doshi's ritual at the altar. Her movements were quietly assured and mindful. We monks stood at our seats, hands clasped in *shashu* at the waist. Slowly the Abbess approached the altar and performed a standing bow, palms pressed together. She made an offering of fragrant wood incense ignited by a small charcoal plug burning in an altar bowl. A slender stream of incense smoke sanctified the zendo air in preparation for the Buddha's teaching, as dharma talks are considered to be.

Next the Abbess laid down her zagu on the altar mat and led the assemblage in three full prostrations. Standing again, she carefully retrieved and folded the zagu, placed it over her left arm, stepped backward from the altar and, turning, walked slowly to her nearby seat on the raised tan. Sitting back onto her zafu, she gracefully lifted her legs from the floor to cross them beneath her robes. As she settled onto her seat, smoothing her okesa over her lap, we monks also sat down facing her to receive the Dharma. Impressed by her elegance and grace, I was eager to hear what she would say. Robes properly arranged, she looked up with a smile, nodded to us and began to speak, softly and with precision.

First the Abbess spoke of our personal "practice bodies." The schedule, she said, allows us to get to know the body of our practice—the Habit Body or Karma Body. This contains ideas about our self, our life story, built on what is already familiar. When things are not working—such as at the beginning of practice period when we are trying to follow a new and demanding schedule—she said, we are not capable of identifying what *will* work for us. We keep bumping into our Karma Body, which has been shaped by past karma and which also creates karma going forward. The schedule forces us to meet our habitual patterns as we try to manipulate circumstances to suit what we've been and done in the past. But because we cannot manipulate the monastery schedule, we feel unable to cope with this new situation.

"Or," she paused and with a twinkle in her eye, said, "we can use the new schedule to liberate ourselves from our habitual karma." Thus the Abbess began to point the way to get through the hardships of the initial weeks of practice period. I saw I was in good hands. I could rely on her guidance. I decided that after each talk I would write notes about what I had heard. As a kinesthetic learner I needed to "handle" new information. Notes would help me absorb the teachings. I also decided to stop trying to control what happened to me. Experience over the next weeks would demonstrate how difficult this ambition was. It would also illustrate how important the Karma Body would be in what I learned at Tassajara.

The five-day monastic week required an entire constellation of new habits I and the other Tangaryo monks had to develop. Not only was the shift from seven to five days initially disorienting, but there were many detailed differences in each schedule that we needed to discern. It would take me two-thirds of practice period to master all four schedules. The monastic week began with three Regular days in a row, followed by one Work day, then a Personal day, and every few weeks, a five-to-seven day Sesshin.

On Regular days, we sat five periods of zazen in the morning, had our meals in the zendo, and studied at 9:00 a.m. for fifty minutes in the dining room. To help us settle into our bodies and calm our minds, the Abbess invited us to sit zazen outdoors for the two mid-morning periods. The mild weather permitted this for almost the entire three months. She instructed us to let the sounds we heard just be sounds, without naming them. To allow the sights come to us rather than to seek them. To let everything be just what it was, including ourselves. When the Karma Body is not in charge, she told us, there is less stress. When we're being the being we are, there is no one doing it. There is Just Being, just the activity. There is no (separate) you. There is only the action—sights, sounds, smells, and so forth. *Relax.*

During morning zazen, we could request private interviews with the Abbess and the three other practice leaders. I was able to meet with the Abbess in dokusan nearly every week, as well as have private interviews with each of the other leaders. The Abbess was especially welcoming. She thought my presence showed the younger monks that Zen can be practiced well into old age.

On the Regular Day afternoons, we worked for three hours at tasks to maintain the monastery and support practice period activities. For the first afternoon work period my job was to clean up the sewing area in the dining hall. Another monk, a young man, was my partner. We sorted and reorganized supplies used for sewing rakusus and okesas. We worked steadily from 1:15 until fifteen minutes before the 4:15 end of work period. Because another task would take more than fifteen minutes to complete, we decided to leave it for the next day and take a coffee break. The Work Leader, an athletic looking, young woman with a determined demeanor, saw us in the coffee area and halted, demanding, "What are you doing here?"

"We're taking our break," I replied.

"No breaks allowed," she growled.

I was alarmed. Weren't breaks required by state employment law? I asked myself. How would I get through work period without at least one short break? I decided I must negotiate up front for permission to take breaks. The next day the Work Leader assigned me to help in the kitchen. After I introduced myself to the Tenzo (Head Cook), I told him I would need a short rest every thirty to forty minutes. I hoped I wasn't violating a monastery rule, but the Tenzo graciously said this would be okay. He would assign a task that could include a pause, making two large sheets of corn bread.

The next afternoon the Work Leader assigned me to work with another student, this time a woman, in the Dish Shack. Our task was to wash, dry, and put away the previous day's enormous quantity of crockery dishes. I wondered why there were so many dishes when we monks ate all our meals oryoki style in the zendo, using, cleaning, and storing our nested bowl sets at our seats. Later I learned that monks with special diets sat through the oryoki meals and afterwards ate their special foods in the kitchen or dining room. I suspected that after the zendo meals, some other monks, especially those having hard, physical work assignments, went to the kitchen for second helpings. Thus the huge quantity of bowls and plates needing to be washed every day.

It took us the full three hours of work period to do twenty-four hours' worth of dishes. I washed and rinsed. My teammate sterilized and dried the dishes and then carted them in crates to the dining room some forty yards away. It was clear that she had the heavier job. I couldn't carry those heavy dish crates. I realized that I couldn't hold up my end on the dish crew or perhaps on any work team. It would be better not to be assigned to one. When I saw the Work Leader next, I told her, "Team work is probably not possible for me, but I can do individual projects, such as reorganizing things—sewing kits or an office or a cabinet."

The following day, however, I was assigned to yet another team. Having participated in work practice at sesshins over the years, I knew the Zen tradition was for the monk to accept any assignment as proof enough that it was needed. Also to not expect to complete the task in the time allowed or to be assigned to the same task the next day in order to complete it. These two work protocols were intended to encourage working selflessly for the community and discourage ego investment in the work. I appreciated this tradition as a good teaching, but taking care of my body had to be the priority. I approached the Work Leader again and said as courteously as I could, "I am not trying to get out of doing work. I very much want to contribute, but I just can't do jobs requiring physical strength or working on a team because I really do need to be able to take short breaks."

The Work Leader nodded. I couldn't tell if she was persuaded. Later that day when I passed her on the pathway, she looked away. I worried that I had become a problem. I felt miserable displeasing anyone, so I remained concerned. Several weeks later I learned that she was then new to the Work Leader role. There was a huge amount of maintenance and repair work to be accomplished that practice period, and she felt responsible for getting it all done. Her discomfort over my needs was not personal; it was organizational, which I could understand. She wanted to do a good job—just as I did. Over time we worked out the jobs I could do and still take breaks. We became friends, and we each discharged our responsibilities well enough.

After the three Regular Days came Work Day on which we worked both morning and afternoon, six hours total. The chief activities were projects to maintain and enhance the physical monastery—gardening, cleaning, constructing, and baking and cooking for special events. On Work Days we were wakened an hour later (4:40 a.m.). We sat one period of zazen, followed by morning service and oryoki breakfast. Then we met in the daily work circle, an open outdoor area next to the zendo building. There the Work Leader assigned us our morning tasks.

On Work Days the Tenzo and kitchen crew prepared delicious buffet lunches, which we ate in the dining room. The lunches offered a greater variety of dishes than our oryoki meals, which were constrained by having to fit easily into monks' small bowls. Work Day lunches included soups, pasta, chili and other spicy bean dishes, homemade bread, fruit, and sometimes something sweet like pudding or a crumble.

Following lunch we returned to the work circle for our afternoon assignments. We worked for another three hours, the last segment of which was cleaning our rooms. The Work Day afternoon ended with personal time of about an hour and a half for exercise and a luxurious soak in the Baths.

But our duties were not complete. Work Day evening began with the *Nenju* ceremony in the zendo, an ancient monastic tradition celebrating the monks' day of work. Prior to the ceremony we monks assembled at the zendo and stood outside on the engawa. For thirty minutes or so, we waited in the dark—and as winter approached, the cold—while the practice period leaders processed in ceremony inside. I never knew what form their ceremony took because I was always outside waiting. And I never asked about it. In my daily fatigue, gradually I lost curiosity about anything I, myself, didn't have to do. This was partly an effect of aging: I had less energy for trying to understand everything going on around me. Plus asking questions seemed to be discouraged. At first I had bristled at the childlike helplessness I felt when I didn't understand what or why things were as they were. But over time I gradually submitted to being ignorant. Eventually I even felt grateful that I didn't have to know or do all that the leaders and more experienced monks did.

This submissive ignorance reminded me of what I had felt twenty years earlier when I lived in Japan. There, understanding only a little Japanese, I was frequently baffled by events: A military parade through town, when Japan supposedly had been unarmed since World War II. Commercial trucks rumbling down the narrow residential alleys blasting slogans in Japanese from loudspeakers as if warning of the apocalypse. Eventually I learned the trucks were merely advertising goods and services. I never found out what the military parade was for. My similar bewilderment about some events at Tassajara became the cocoon of ignorance I inhabited more and more as time passed. As in Japan, I found I could survive without knowing all the nuances.

The Nenju ceremony in the evening of Work Days occurred six or seven times over the three months, every five-day week in which we did not have a sesshin. The first two times, three of my over-fifty-five Tangaryo dorm mates and I were greatly affronted to be left standing for thirty minutes outside the zendo at the end of our hard day's work. We were tired. But once the monastery leaders finished whatever it was they did inside, the rest of us monks entered. We offered incense at the altar and then walked around the zendo single file, half crouched with hands in prayer pose. This ceremony, called a *jundo,* honored everyone for working hard that day.

As we reached each of the practice leaders at their seats, we stopped and bowed more deeply, then moved to our own seats. There we stood and bowed in turn to each successive monk as they passed us. The jundo walk was amusing, snaking around the room, half bent over. At the end of the procession when everyone had returned to their cushions, the *Kokyo* (chant leader) called out, "Ho—San!" His voice rose in a glissando and volume from the first syllable to the second one, which he delivered as a loud, high yelp or whoop. Both exotic and amusing to hear.

Work Day was followed by a Personal Day, which had the same schedule but without work assignments. We woke an hour later than on Regular Schedule days, sat one period of zazen and had morning service in the zendo. Following that we had a fulsome buffet breakfast on crockery in the dining room. I found our zendo oryoki meals both tasty and nourishing, but on Personal Days we had treats like scrambled eggs or soufflés, pancakes with syrup or biscuits or fresh breads, whole fruits, and glasses of juice. The Personal Day menus varied except in their deliciousness.

After breakfast on Personal Days we were free until evening service at 5:30 p.m. I quickly learned to make the most of my free time, catching up on personal tasks, exercising, and relaxing. After breakfast, along with most everyone else, I went to the kitchen and quickly packed a lunch. The cooks put out an abundant array of breads, cheeses, vegetables, fruits, and cookies for us to take. After storing my lunch bag in the monks' refrigerator outside the dining room, I dashed up to the laundry shed with five days of dirty clothes. My goal was to snag a washtub before too many other monks did.

Clothes washing was an adventure in itself. First we filled a five-gallon bucket with wonderfully hot water. Next we added powdered environmentally safe soap supplied by Tassajara. Then we used a cone-shaped, metal plunger on a broom handle (like a plumber's helper) to drive our clothes up and down in the bucket. The soapy water quickly turned an astonishing dark gray. Our clothes weren't dirty from heavy use. It was the mountain's silty dust that penetrated even our undergarments. After rinsing, we squeezed out the water using an old-fashioned hand-cranked roller and hung our garments out to dry on nearby clotheslines. The weather that year remained warm until December, so my clothes almost always dried completely by 4:00 p.m. I was able to wash, dry, and put them away on the same day. This outcome gave me a satisfying sense of control over my life—once every five days.

After laundry, I could move on to leisure activities. Being able to choose what to do was a palpable luxury. I usually spent some time writing letters (by hand, of course; computers not allowed). The mail was picked up at the top of Tassajara Road and delivered two or three times a week. By the second week I began to receive letters from Zen friends. I had asked them to support me in this big effort, and I was very grateful to hear from them. They cheered me on.

On Personal Days, many monks hiked out of the deep, narrow valley to work out the kinks from zazen. For the first six weeks, I didn't have the energy for hiking, but I did longer sessions of yoga than on Regular Days. The large yoga room in the Conference Center was equipped with a full array of yoga props—mats, bolsters, straps, blankets, blocks. Throughout the three months, I kept up a daily yoga practice. I also took advantage of the outdoor swimming pool—such a luxury in the midst of our strict life. On Personal Days I almost always found time for a good swim, not as frequent or as long as my swims back home, but refreshing. The water consisted of icy cold layers from Tassajara Creek and streams of hot water from the mineral springs. If I scampered through the cold streaks into the warm ones, the water was tolerable. I was one of only a handful of monks who used the pool, and I was grateful to have it.

On Personal Days I could spend more time than usual at the Baths. After removing one's shoes and storing them on shelves outside the building, the ritual was to light a stick of incense at the small outside altar and bow three times. Before entering the hot bath pool, one washed in the communal shower. I always luxuriated in the shower, washing off not only the days' grime but also the stress of perpetually rushing to keep the practice schedule. Following a generous cleansing, I stepped, pristine, into the deep mineral Bath. First I sat on one of the pool shelves for two or three minutes, immersed up to my chin. Then I slowly walked around, head just above the surface, to feel the gentle massage as my movement stirred the hot mineral water. Finally I lay down on a shelf, head propped against the poolside to let the body float. I could never stay in the bath for more than seven or eight minutes. The water, 105 to 108 degrees F, was too hot to remain longer, but even these few minutes were deeply restorative.

The women's Bath had a small outdoor hot pool overlooking Tassajara Creek where one could enjoy the creek's burbling water and the riparian greenery. There was also a large wooden deck area for sunning. The *pièce de résistance* of the Baths was a natural steam room, a stone grotto fed by mineral spring water that trickled down the walls and dripped hotly from above. It was like a cave smelling of rich earth and plant life. Sitting alone inside the grotto, I imagined myself an ascetic monk in an ancient Irish abbey, wickedly relishing bodily pleasures.

I was always rejuvenated by my Personal Day enjoyment of the Baths. Dressed again, moving slowly, I would leave the building, bow three times at the altar, put on my shoes, and stroll along the musical Tassajara Creek back to the dorm, all senses satisfied. Some monks devoted Personal days to catching up on their sleep. Given my habitual fatigue, I knew I should sleep too, but I hated to waste a minute of the freedom to choose and vary my activities. I craved variety. Choosing, itself, was restorative.

The final variation of Days was the schedule for Sesshins, consecutive days of intensive practice, of which we had four during the practice period. The wake-up bell for sesshins was 3:50 a.m. Early on, I learned I needed a cup of caffeinated coffee to stay awake through the sesshin morning. I set the alarm for 3:40 a.m. in order to add to the morning preparations a quick dash down to the coffee machine near the dorm. This was my only exception to eschewing caffeine at Tassajara.

Sesshins included eleven periods of zazen each day and only seventy minutes of afternoon work assignments. Sesshin Days required strong effort in zazen, but they were easier for me than Regular and Work Days because the activities were fewer and simpler: Sit, walk, bow, chant, eat, and eventually sleep. Also, after the first sesshin, the Abbess exempted me from the work period so I could rest, greatly easing my way through the long days of zazen.

Five weeks into practice period, our first sesshin began, five days long. The first day my head was heavy, my mind aimless, depressed. I was unable to concentrate: Torpor. I slumped on my cushion, desperate to lie down. I tried to practice returning to the breath but repeatedly lost focus. I craved diversion, "stories," but I couldn't focus even on those. Sitting outside during late morning zazen, I gazed at the sycamore tree above me. The small-leafed branches seemed so complicated, opposing and crossing each other like agitated dendrites. Their form seemed greatly in excess of efficient functioning. Was complexity the nature of everything—including, perhaps, the mind? No wonder it was so hard to settle down. Bleary eyed, I waited for the bell ending outdoor zazen.

Back in the zendo, the Tassajara Administrative Director, a fully authorized priest and one of the practice leaders, gave a dharma talk that put my frazzled mind back in order. She offered an antidote for when we were struggling in zazen or during our daily routine: Use the Four Noble Truths as practice instructions, she said:

- *Suffering,* or *Dukkha, means being out of balance.* How do we experience our life out of balance? What do we get upset about? We have to get to know suffering. Attend just to this, our experience. Notice. Be present with it. Look at how suffering arises.
- *What causes our suffering?* Observe that it is our reaction to what arises in our experience that causes our suffering.
- *How do we end our suffering?* Let go of clinging to our views and past experiences, and see that our suffering dissolves.
- *There is a way to live beyond suffering.* Cultivate the Eight-fold Path, the eight practices that train the mind toward liberation and enlightenment.

The Director also offered tips for dealing with difficulties that arise during zazen:

- *When you encounter torpor or boredom, go deeper.* What is the quality of boredom? How do you know you are bored? What is in your body? What thoughts? What resistance? What's happening now? What is it you can't stand? Be a naturalist of your own experience to understand it. It will change because of your attention.

- *Afflicted states such as resentment, envy, or anger are buried, scary places.* Acknowledge and gently investigate them. If you encounter a part of yourself you don't want to accept, go slowly. How much can you sit with and not drown? Negotiate with yourself on this.
- *Zazen posture is good for containing strong emotion.* Sitting up with some energy can be a container. We can feel safe within the posture and allow afflictive emotions to arise.
- *When you encounter difficulties in zazen, ask questions.* What's happening now that's difficult? What is the perfect instruction I need now? Follow this instruction.

I was grateful for these wise, practical teachings, yet later that day I fell into grave doubt about having been ordained. I observed other priests at Tassajara behaving so "professionally," their robes and okesas elegant, their demeanors composed. What had I been thinking to become a priest? I didn't have their self-assurance. Eventually I might learn some priest craft, but I feared I lacked aptitude.

Comparisons, I knew, were odious: they only served to separate us from one another, making us feel diminished. My thoughts drifted on. I was experiencing self-doubt partly because I was sitting next to a priest who was punctilious about all priest craft. She knew all the correct forms and procedures. She instructed me often on them in the zendo. Miming, she pointed out the errors I made in turning on my cushion to face the wall, in placing chopsticks on the middle oryoki bowl, or in holding the Buddha bowl over the food pot offered by the server. I learned a lot from her, but as time went on, we both grew weary of our roles—she, impatient with my mistakes, and I, resentful of her gratuitous tutelage.

On the morning of the next to the last day of sesshin, I was so tired I fell seriously asleep during the third period of zazen (5:30–6:00 a.m.). It was not just the body that was tired. I felt exhausted mentally. I could barely move. Later that morning I met in practice discussion with the Director. I described my mental exhaustion.

"I feel like a heap," I said, "a beaten down heap." She responded, "Please inquire into this mind state and others that occur during zazen. What do they feel like? Where are they located? What do they tell you? Become mentally active," she told me. Pausing a few moments, she said: "Visualize a quiet pool to which all the animals come to drink. Invite your mind state to come and drink too. Be sympathetic to it, help it to relax and calm down." I thanked her for her kind advice and got ready to depart. "Remember to intervene when you get lost like this," she said. "Investigate. Be interested. Discover."

Back in zazen, it occurred to me that I could just enjoy myself. After all, this was my *life* I was living. It wasn't some prerequisite for a future, real thing. What would it take to accept what I was experiencing? Later that afternoon I petitioned the universe for happiness and freedom from suffering. I visualized the calm pool the Director had described and invited my disheveled mind to its edge. In the water's reflection, the mind looked like a black tangle of wiry hair. But as it contemplated the peaceful pool, it calmed down, transforming into a curled-up hedgehog, a harmless, cuddly creature. Maybe my mind would relax further and even become kind to me. Could I lighten up?

I had finally learned the ropes at Tassajara, but I was not enjoying myself. What was the value of this training? I thought of the Outward Bound program, which pushes participants to do physical activities they would not try on their own. Outward Bound leaders don't teach by giving the participants information. Students have to learn by doing. Walking across a tightrope high above the ground is the most famous (to me, terrifying) exercise. Maybe Tassajara pushed us up against whatever limitations we brought with us to help us go beyond them. We came there knowing how to do zazen, quiet our minds, and work with the abstruse concepts of Buddhism. What we didn't know was how to break out of whatever personal limitations we had locked ourselves into over our lifetimes. Only by being pushed up against the chains of our delusions and neurotic Karma Bodies might we be able to change. The hope was that we would transform. The fear was that we would disintegrate. At least that was my fear.

Chapter Ten

Community as Mirror

As we moved into the second half of practice period, the leaders introduced the theme of Living in Community in their dharma talks. Each one urged us to examine our fixed views and habitual reactions in relation to others. When we saw we had made up a story about someone's motive or meaning, they advised us to "Just drop it" because it was only our story. We don't really know what is going on for another person, they said. We concoct stories to explain to ourselves what's happening. But stories aren't based on full information, so they're likely wrong. Also, they take us out of the present moment, which is where we want to stay because only there can we be free from suffering.

Our study of community living was not about how to talk or solve problems together. We were to observe how and what *we* thought about others. We were to study how our thoughts and feelings affected our relationship with others and thus affected the whole community. Negative assessments of others (He's too bossy) color our expectations and behavior (Don't tell me what to do). Being introverted by nature, I dropped easily into this self-examination. Outwardly busy following the schedule, inwardly, I was intensely focused on studying the Self, as Dogen Zenji had taught. What was it like for me to live with others? What assumptions and habits around relating with people did I have? How did my responses to others affect their behavior and my own? I discovered much I hadn't known before.

Practice period put us Tangaryo monks under a lot of stress. We were in silence eighteen hours a day and asleep the other six. The daily schedule was rigorous. Almost every day we had to learn new and often complex tasks. The program was challenging. The silence we kept gave us the space first to notice our reactions, then to reflect on their validity or error, and ultimately to revise and/or release our reactivity. These were unprecedented opportunities, though emotionally intense ones.

For the first month every day we interacted with people we had just met. Naturally, we used whatever socialization modes and skills we had developed in the past, perhaps long years past. We brought different expectations and behavioral habits to our relationships with different categories of people—the leaders, work teammates, dorm mates, and the handful of monks with whom we developed friendships in the little free time we had. I brought certain advantages to this situation. I had professional experience studying group dynamics, leadership, and communication problems in groups. I had attended many residential Zen sesshins over the years. I knew how to share sleeping quarters and work tasks with strangers. I also brought two disadvantages. I was decades older than the other monks, and I had lived alone for the previous thirty years. I might be less aware and practiced in interpreting and flexing with other people's behaviors. Silent interactions with other community members provided many opportunities to observe my habitual assumptions about myself in relation to others.

I shouldn't have been surprised that my habitual—Karma Body—reactions weren't always effective. I discovered that my strategy for integrating into a new group was to insist on "being helpful." I hadn't been aware of this habit before. I became aware of it now only because it didn't work well. If it had worked, I might never have seen it. In our silence, perhaps my intended helpfulness was not evident to others. Being helpful may depend more on language than on one's actions. Whatever the case, when I saw what I was attempting to do, I was startled. Was I trying to manipulate people into accepting me? If so, I might be interfering with them, something I did not want to do. I was excited to realize I could discard this habit. Of course I would help when asked, but I would no longer expect that helping would bring me acceptance.

The lesson in this discovery was to examine my intention: Was I trying to get others to accept me? Or was I responding to the genuine need of another for help? Most of the jobs we did—cooking, cleaning, weeding, etc.—were assigned and limited to single tasks to be accomplished in specific periods of time. Because the division of labor was so specifically defined, we did not often need to help each other. Usually we just needed to work next to each other. Tassajara was a model of organizational efficiency.

Another hidden habit surfaced during the first two weeks when I struggled with the Work Leader over the types of jobs she assigned me. At first when I couldn't persuade her to give me work I felt I could do, I concluded I was the cause of her grouchy response. Later when I learned that she was under pressure to get a lot of work done, I realized it was her mission, not me, that caused her frustration. This led me to seeing another bad habit of mine: feeling responsible for other people's reaction to me. It probably originated in the Karma Body I had constructed back when I was ostracized as an adolescent. Since then—sixty-five years!—I had believed that I alone was the cause of problems in interactions. How absurd.

The silence of monastic life became the petri dish in which my conditioning around relationships bloomed. I was astonished to see it, and thrilled: I might be able to discard other lifelong habits that had limited my choices and created suffering. Fully engaged in practice period now, I also saw for the first time that everyone's behavior is influenced by past conditioning. Their behavior toward me could not be simply in reaction to my behavior. I could not know why they behaved as they did, but I could empathize with them because we are all conditioned. I could stop feeling separate and inadequate.

Just as these insights grew out of interactions with other monks, training in ceremonial forms exposed my strengths and weaknesses for learning. The particulars of zendo forms at Tassajara were precise and often without obvious reason for how they were to be performed. I found it hard to remember all the details about when and how to strike a bell or drum in a ceremonial role. Even the daily, repeated forms for bowing and moving together and for eating oryoki style had nuances I'm sure I didn't properly perform or even perceive. The rub for me was making mistakes in front of people I didn't yet know or trust. I wanted to be accepted in the community—probably everyone wanted this. I recognized that making mistakes helps us drop our self-centeredness and perfectionism. Still, I dreaded repeated public failure.

I blundered onward. The schedule propelled us all forward. The teachings provided by the practice period leaders encouraged me through my more painful training moments. They helped put in perspective the strong and unexpected conditioned reactions and emotions monastic training was revealing to me.

In a dharma talk, the Abbess pointed out that our perception of others was ninety-eight percent just *our* interpretation of the other person's actions, not the reality of their actions. We perceive only a tiny part of what is really going on. So, she told us, treat everything and everyone as sacred, as Buddha. We can't change anything in the other person, but we do help each other by completely taking care of our *own* lives. I was thunderstruck by this statement. All my life I had been focused on wresting acceptance from others. Focusing more on my own behavior had never occurred to me.

The Abbess elaborated: Our own wholehearted practice helps others. As individuals we are both totally alone and totally interconnected. She asked us to practice opening our hearts to liberate ourselves from our Karma Bodies. I reflected on these wise words and how they corroborated the insights I was having about my conditioning. I began to disentangle my habitual self from the current circumstances. My reactivity to the imperatives of the schedule loosened.

One day during the noon oryoki meal, I suddenly realized I was feeling agitated. This was ironic, given that I was sitting quietly waiting to eat. I was watching the meal serving team moving quickly around the zendo in, to me, mysteriously complex patterns and at a speed I could never achieve, were I on a serving team. I saw I was comparing myself to these younger monks and feeling a failure. I decided to stop watching them, to just keep my gaze downward, as in zazen. Actually, the downward gaze was recommended as a way to keep the practice whenever we were with others. No longer watching the servers, immediately I felt calmer. With this simple adjustment, body and mind became tranquil.

The next day my mind returned to struggling. I hadn't slept well, and throughout early morning zazen I fell asleep repeatedly, tipping over and jerking back to remain upright. It was in this exhausted state that later I listened with the community during study period to an audiotape sent us by Steve Stuckey, Abbot of San Francisco Zen Center. Abbot Steve had just been diagnosed with pancreatic cancer and sent this recorded message to Tassajara to say he was meeting this devastating diagnosis head on. It was a sobering and admirable communication to his Tassajara students, who loved and revered him. They were understandably shocked.

In my sleep-deprived, muddled half-consciousness, however, I couldn't focus on the Abbot's courageous words. Instead, my mind jumped to my problems, my unsettled mind— how in zazen I wasn't able to focus. How I was feeling so frustrated. If I knew and understood more what was happening, I might be able to relax. Instead, I was just blundering along. I hated this feeling. On and on, I silently complained. I recognized it was truly reprehensible to be preoccupied with myself when Abbot Steve was dying and was so compassionately sharing this sad news with his students. In my frazzled mind it was all about me, me, me.

Horrified about what this selfishness said about my mental state, I decided I must be more assertive regarding the special accommodations I needed for resting. I asked to see the Tanto for practice discussion. I wanted to remind him of our phone conversation prior to practice period concerning my physical limitations. Tim had also talked with him about my needs, as he promised he would. Now that I was getting my bearings at Tassajara, I wanted to clarify what would work for me and get the Tanto's support. Asking again for help was embarrassing, but I knew from my experience in the hierarchical work world that I must speak up or I would not get what I needed.

The Tanto was energetic and humorous while maintaining an authoritative manner, one I sometimes found intimidating. We met in his dokusan room, a tiny space. It had room for only two zabutons touching and facing each other, plus a small area for a bowing zabuton in front of the Buddha altar. When seated, our faces were only two feet apart. I had to refocus my eyes and take a deep breath to feel comfortable. Our discussion went smoothly enough, though, about my needs and limitations. Because I felt the Work Leader had not understood them, I asked the Tanto to intervene so I could be assigned jobs I could actually do.

The Tanto agreed to speak with her. While I had his attention, I also told him about needing one or two naps every day to make up for some of the sleep I didn't get at night. "I'm finding that I am most tired at around 9 a.m. and again after lunch, so I have been trying to insert naps during those times. What should I say on the Tenken Sheet when I sign out multiple times each day?"

"Just write, 'Rest, as per the Tanto,'" he replied. "I will inform the Tenken monks that this means you are in your room, napping." I felt satisfied that he understood and agreed to what I should do. I thanked him for his help.

I had been chewing on another complaint, one I kept to myself. We monks were being rigorously trained in zendo forms, comportment, and obedience to the schedule. However, many aspects of the ceremonial forms, themselves—the choreography for serving oryoki meals, the multiple bells and drums for services and special ceremonies—were far more complex than my home sangha could emulate. What was the point of learning all these details when I would never use them again? Like the teenager who doesn't see the point of learning math or history, I felt a sullen resistance rising in me.

What I was resisting, though I didn't realize it at the time, was a growing feeling of incompetence and a fear of failing publicly. Over a long life, I had figured out how to use my natural aptitudes to learn skills and pursue activities I could succeed at, and to avoid activities at which I would probably fail. A perfectly sensible approach in our competitive American life, I thought. It more or less assured the appearance that I was "a success." Clever.

At Tassajara, I was required to learn things outside my natural learning modes and abilities. This was tough, and worse, I couldn't get out of it. Here was another opportunity for self-awareness. I wanted to look good, but mostly I couldn't make that happen here. The best I could do was to try hard, though there were times due to fatigue or frustration when even that was too much. Plus I resented being in the ignominious position of having to try when I didn't want to. Ouch! Here was a conditioning pattern I would learn more about as practice period continued: Although I could find ways to appear to be knowledgeable and even wise, appearance was not the complete reality.

In retrospect, I see that some of the struggle I had with the training at Tassajara was due to old age. I was no longer able to do what even a few years earlier I could have done readily: physically move quickly, absorb new information easily, and act confidently in the presence of strangers. I felt ashamed of being slower and less competent now, and I was anxious not to reveal my inadequacies further. It is common for elders to feel embarrassed when, unexpectedly, we can't fulfill a commitment we have made. Eventually we learn our new limits and choose or adjust our goals and activities. But I was slammed up against Tassajara's demanding schedule and believed further adjustments were not possible. This made monastic life particularly stressful. Finding my usual competence impossible, by the end of the first month, I silently blamed the schedule and the "system" for my unhappiness. I loved Personal Days because I could choose what to do all day long. But I had no choice on Regular or Work Days. For a while both days became odious to me. My thinking had become the *cause* of my suffering—just as the Buddha taught.

In the very accessible book, *What is Zen?*, Norman Fischer and Sue Moon succinctly capture the practice issue I was then grappling with, though I did not understand it at the time. Norman acknowledges that Zen teachers should not force their students to do something—

> inappropriately or outrageously scary. . . . [just] to stretch the student . . . yet we do have to go into those walled-off scary areas of our heart; we do have to make peace with and go beyond what we most fear, including, and especially, our fear of death. . . . [This] does involve our letting go of everything. As long as we determine that in our study of Zen we will permit this but not that, go this far but no further, we will remain imprisoned in ourselves (Fischer and Moon 2016, 106).

Going beyond my established limits was painful but necessary.

By mid-October, five weeks into practice period, it was consistently cold in the early mornings but warm, even hot, in the afternoons. By this time, I had had three or four dokusan meetings with the Abbess, who helped and supported me. One morning as I entered the dokusan room, the Abbess was sitting in a chair rather than on her zafu as she ordinarily did. She gestured toward a chair opposite her and asked if I would be more comfortable sitting there. I was touched that she probably had noticed I had been struggling on my zafu during zazen. From that time on, she made that special accommodation and we sat in chairs to talk.

Once seated, I spoke about my concern that day, a recent lack of focus in zazen. After I described the experience, she advised putting a little more energy into my sitting posture and mudra. See if that focused my mind, woke me up. She also recommended Theravaden Master Ajahn Chah's teachings on focusing the mind on the breath, noticing it at the nose, the upper chest and the abdomen. When a wholesome thought arises, follow it for a while. But if the thought is unwholesome, just drop it and return to the breath. Focus on direct experience—sensations and feelings—not on thoughts. This was a basic teaching I had known for years, but its simplicity was perfect for my increasingly confounded mind. Despite my recent appreciation that we can't know what causes other people's behavior, I continued to be distracted by speculations about others and their motives. I would have to intercede in such thoughts again and again. This very simple practice of watching the breath calmed and encouraged me in this task.

It turned out that breath work was also the perfect focus for the next few days. I came down with the miserable, hacking cough going around the sangha. I was advised to keep away from others so as not to spread the germ more widely. I stayed in my little room for two full days and nights. I napped and watched my breath and napped again. I coughed, I ached, I lost appetite and energy, just as others before me had. Despite the troubles I had been having with the schedule, ironically, now I felt lonely and wanted to rejoin the other monks. Fortunately, the Tenken monks brought me meals and offered to help in any way they could. I hadn't been aware that patient care was part of their job. I was touched by their compassion.

The illness provided the opportunity, finally, to assess my room. Lying in bed without the energy to do anything else, I peered closely at the four bare, white walls. They were smudged and marred by the remnants of tape and tack holes where previous monks had displayed photos or pictures. I had not put up anything. At home I had paintings and pleasant furnishings in all the rooms, but here I seemed to want no distraction from the severity of practice. I liked the tall, screened window next to the bed. Its brown metal Venetian mini-blinds were sloppy and dusty, but they provided privacy and fresh air at night for sleeping. I looked down on nearby cabins and the small bridge over the dry Cabarga Creek bed, which in the winter carries storm water down the mountainside into Tassajara Creek. The twin-sized bed was directly beneath the window, its length exactly the width of the room. The foam rubber mattress on a plywood platform on which I slept in a sleeping bag was surprisingly comfortable. There was enough room beneath the bed to store two suitcases, an economy of space I much appreciated.

Hooks and hangers and drawers accommodated my few items of clothing, robes, and priest's paraphernalia. A creaking, armless wooden chair provided seating for a visitor. A small oak chest stored smaller items—vitamins, prescriptions, underwear, socks, and t-shirts. On top were a small lamp, the only light source in the room, my alarm clock, and small notebooks. In the communal bathroom a couple of doors away, I had a drawer for toiletries. In all, my residence was unadorned but orderly, a monkish refuge from what would become my increasingly turbulent mind. The decor said, Focus, pay attention, do what's necessary.

In fact Tassajara felt so challenging that instinctively I seemed to want nothing to distract me from learning and following the schedule. In the tradition of the monk, I had left home. I had not brought it with me. Analogous to the four walls close around me, my focus was narrow, specific, on just the tasks I was required to learn and execute. My mind, like my small room, encapsulated my experience. The silence we kept led naturally to keeping to myself. I stayed out of the way—somewhat as I had as a child during (rare) family crises, such as when my big sister's boyfriend got lost all night in the High Sierras and everyone feared he had been eaten by a bear. Or when Mother thought Dad had been unfaithful to her on a fishing trip, and Dad broke down in tears in front my two sisters and me. In such upsetting moments, I took to my bed, not wanting to be in the way. Now afraid I was not up to the demands of practice period, my instinct was to simplify, retract. And as we would be advised, not to interfere with others by making up stories about them in our heads. In these ways, my experience of Tassajara became almost entirely interior—confined but rich.

In a few days I did recover from being sick and rejoined the other monks. The irony of being glad to return to the stressful schedule was not lost on me. But I was growing used to these frequent, contradictory mind states, both pleasant and unpleasant. Monastery life went on. One late afternoon, I mistakenly left a warm, black fleece shirt at the Baths. I considered going back for it, but I was too tired to walk down the long path and back a second time. The next day when I went to retrieve it, it was gone. At our daily Work Circle that week during General Announcements, I asked if anyone had seen it, but no one had. I had heard complaints that things sometimes disappeared from the clotheslines. We Tangaryo students had been advised to mark our clothing with our names. I wondered if the shirt had been stolen. As my one warm outer garment, it was important now that the mornings were colder. I didn't like suspecting that someone in our community might have taken it. It scared me a little to think that one of us might not be trustworthy. When I asked about it again another day, two monks offered to lend me warm shirts of their own. Touched, I gratefully accepted a gray cashmere sweater from another Tangaryo student, a vivid and stylish young woman. Her sweater fit well and kept me cozy throughout practice period. At the end, when we said goodbye, I told her I would take her sweater home, wash it, and mail it back to her. But she insisted that I keep it.

Her generosity, and the kindness of the Tenken monks who delivered my meals when I was sick, stood out like bright jewels against the dark fabric of our strict, monastic life. Their compassion made me realize both how alone I sometimes felt, and how powerful living with others was. The silence and the continual, mostly wordless encounters with community members, all but two of whom I had never met before, presented many opportunities to observe how I related with others. These silent encounters taught me lessons I wish I had learned much earlier in life, but ones still useful for my remaining years.

Chapter Eleven

The Mirror Cracks

Throughout October I mused on the Abbess's teaching on Just Being what and as we are, whatever we are experiencing. I wondered if my "assignment" for practice period might be *not* striving to do what everyone else was doing, but just doing/being what I could. I had spent a lifetime trying to hold up my end so I would be accepted. The concept of Just Being was uncomfortable, but worth investigating.

Just Being reminded me of Dave's annoyance that I was always so active. This was a painful issue for nearly our entire marriage, one I never understood. Now unable to keep up with the other monks, I was irritated by their high energy, as Dave must have been by mine.

In dokusan with the Abbess in an attempt to Just Be myself, I confessed I had not been feeling especially spiritual recently. I was intrigued by her response: Perhaps long years of Zen practice had infused my daily life so fully with Zen Mind that I might not feel anything special about practicing. I might be Just Being.

On the final evening of our first sesshin, we monks participated in a Shosan ceremony. In this ritual, the sesshin teacher sits in front of the altar. Each student goes to her, bows, and before the assembled students, asks a sincere question about his or her practice. All the monks asked interesting questions, and the Abbess's answers were insightful. When it was my turn, I asked, "How can I face my fears?"

"Set your intention every morning to get acquainted with your fear, and every evening to evaluate your experience," the Abbess replied. "Not to judge how well you have done but to track your efforts in meeting and exploring fears." A gentle yet practical answer to ponder as later I lay down to sleep.

That night I had a powerful dream. In it I opened the door to leave my small Tassajara dorm room. As I stepped over the threshold, an enormous leopard burst out from under an adjacent, closed door, which in the dream I recognized as the door to the basement in my childhood home. The leopard lunged at me, snarling and clawing ferociously. Terrified, I leapt backward into my room and slammed the door, shutting the leopard out. I woke up, gasping for air. I had asked the Abbess what to do about fear, and in my dream Fear jumped right out at me.

The next day was a Personal Day, so we didn't have to maintain silence. After breakfast I told the Abbess about the dream. We shook our heads in amazement that my question had evoked such a powerful dream. Later that morning as I attended to laundry and room cleaning, I puzzled over the dream's meaning. It was so vivid. There must be something important about it. I also realized that though I had asked about fear, I hadn't been conscious that I was feeling afraid of anything at Tassajara. Frustrated, confused, annoyed these first weeks. But afraid?

I couldn't remember much about the dream leopard's appearance, its color or spots. What impressed me was that I hadn't known that such a creature was lurking in the basement. Or even that there was a basement. Now, suddenly, it was lunging at me. Shocking. And magical: it had slipped under the closed basement door and then instantly returned to full size. Did it mean to harm me? Or did it simply want to make fear conscious?

During the first weeks at Tassajara I had worried about finding my place—getting job assignments I could do physically and permission to rest every day. I did fear that if I could not make these things happen, I couldn't take care of myself as I believed I needed to. Maybe unconsciously I feared I might be a victim of the monastery program and be told to leave. Or was the leopard trying to warn me about something deeper? I was learning that some long-held assumptions about myself and my place in the world could be erroneous. The Abbess's teachings about our Karma Body or "self-story" suggested I had a subterranean story going on, and practice period was a good time to unearth it. Was the leopard here to enlighten me?

The first day following sesshin, back on Regular Schedule, I was so tired during early morning zazen that I nearly pitched headfirst off my chair. This was a nap emergency. I signed out of the zendo, went to my room, and slept during late morning zazen. When I awoke, I realized I had missed lunch. Was I in trouble? Anxiety about breaking rules appeared to be a big piece of my conditioning. Most of the time I managed to do as I was told, but it was fear that drove me. Worth noting. Once fully awake, I realized I could explain, and I could go to the kitchen to get some food, just as students with special diets regularly did.

I worked most of that afternoon's three-hour work period reorganizing and cleaning the First Aid cabinet in one of the supply cabins. This was an engaging job because it was important to have medical supplies in good, accessible order. It called on organizational skills for sorting and labeling and grouping the many first aid items, some of which I knew nothing about. Some research was needed. Best of all, it was a job I could do alone and not impose on a teammate when I needed to rest. I was happy to have the assignment.

We were six weeks into practice period now. The other monks seemed to have adjusted to the schedule, but I was feeling further and further behind. I wondered again what the leopard dream symbolized. Maybe it didn't represent fear, itself, but a response to being afraid—anger? Maybe the leopard was not menacing me. Maybe it was coming to my defense. It was true that my analytical skills were of little use at Tassajara. Perhaps now that my survival might be at stake, I needed a primitive energy—leopard energy.

More often now I noticed I was annoyed, even irritable. That evening in the zendo, the unfriendly seatmate on my left seemed to shrink away especially strongly, as one might do when the only seat left on the bus is next to someone noticeably smelly. I reflected on her cold behavior when we passed on the walkway outdoors. I would smile and nod 'hello' to her, but she would either ignore me or barely respond with a half-second glance before looking past me. Why did she behave this way? Sitting next to someone so rejecting every day was getting to me. Did I fear I would be annihilated if I wasn't accepted? I did want my existence acknowledged. After all, we were in this together. Maybe I did feel threatened.

Was it just ego that was hurting? But if ego is just a construct, what did it matter if someone didn't acknowledge it? It was empty of meaning. Maybe the message was that I had *no self* to recognize. According to the teachings I was absorbing at Tassajara, if she rejected me, it was her *concept* of me she was rejecting, not actually me. I did not need to allow her behavior to color my experience. I could just practice—which also would give her the space to practice.

It didn't occur to me until long after practice period that this monk might have been practicing the monastic rule of silence, which could include not giving nonverbal gestures of acknowledgement as well as vocal silence. My failure to consider this at the time underscores the depth of my need for acceptance to feel safe.

Toward the end of October it finally rained—a palpable relief to me from worrying that the drought might cause a fire. A little cheered for a change, and still curious about how things worked at Tassajara, I took an opportunity during late afternoon free time to speak with one of the Doan-ryo monks about the sutras we chanted in the zendo. The resident monks seemed to be such accomplished chanters. I wondered if they were required to memorize the chants.

"No, people just learn them by doing them every day," the monk told me.

"How do they learn to do the unusual syncopated chants? Did they have special instructions?"

"No, they just pick up how to do them by listening to the monks who know them. That's how we do things at Tassajara. People aren't taught to do anything; they just observe and pick up how things are done." He seemed bemused by my questions.

This description of the pedagogical approach at Tassajara surprised me, but it might explain why so little information was offered during the first month. Were they emulating the Japanese educational practice of imitation? Surely, that could not meet everyone's learning needs. The U.S. educational system had long practiced multiple ways to support student learning—visual, auditory, kinesthetic approaches—so everyone could be successful through their natural mode. Here, having only a brief oral description and demonstration of how to ring bells or hit drums before having to perform on them seemed to ensure that new monks made many mistakes.

I understood that making mistakes might help us break down egocentrism and perfectionism. However—annoyance rising as I continued thinking— this approach could have an unintended consequence. Due to the embarrassment new monks might feel making mistakes before the community (I certainly did), we might become emotionally dependent on the practice leaders: To learn how to do things correctly, we had to watch them closely and continuously. This seemed inappropriate in an adult learning setting.

I did not share my speculations, but after our conversation an inner voice snarled, "Is this a cult?" Startled that after so many years of Zen practice this suspicion would occur to me, I immediately redirected my thoughts to more rational reflections. Did the Tassajara system "select" for certain types of people? Traditionally, of course, monastery training was for younger people, who would not yet have refined or ingrained their modes of learning. For an older person like me, who had developed effective learning strategies over many years, this sink-or-swim method was a shock. It might also be tough for those who were not auditory learners or lacked aptitude for detail, or who needed to understand *why* things were done as they were, not just *what* was to be done.

Possibly my annoyance about the teaching method was related to fear, which I continued to study. I recalled that the summer before coming to Tassajara, I worked up a big fear that a forest fire might occur while I was there. Tassajara had had two life-threatening fires in years past, and, given the current severe drought in California, fire was an acknowledged danger. Was I hoping unconsciously to avoid going to practice period where I (myself) might fail? So that I would be fully prepared (wanting to know the worst) before going, all summer long I followed two online weather and fire websites. I read a good book about the 2008 Tassajara fire: Colleen Morton Busch's *Fire Monks* (2011) described the courage of the Tassajara residents, chief among them Abbot Steve Stuckey, who saved Tassajara that year. I saw that I would be of little help if fire threatened the monastery. I was no longer physically strong enough to do what the Fire Monks accomplished. So I had worried before arriving, and I was worrying still. Was I just displacing my anxiety about failing at Tassajara onto the possibility of a fire? My mind went round and round. One of the aims of Zen practice is to break down our ubiquitous cognitive thinking so that we can directly experience the present moment, but I was beginning to worry that my mind itself was breaking.

On October 31, Halloween arrived in the outside world. I celebrated it as the halfway mark of practice period. At 8 a.m. I took part with several other monks in a thirty-minute training for the *Shoten* role—ringing bells and hitting a drum after evening zazen and before the next morning's zazen. This was the first zendo role I had been invited to learn. Like other ceremonial trainings, it was rapid fire. Later, during work period, I met with Eyu to practice the role. She was a Tangaryo monk with whom I had traveled to Tassajara in the van from SFZC. Tall and slender, Eyu was both beautiful and modest in manner. She was an avid hiker and escaped the monastery compound at every opportunity to hike the rough surrounding terrain. At the end of the Shoten training, she suggested that we rehearse the role together. She must have seen my growing confusion and terror. I was grateful for her offer, and her method suited me well. We physically walked through the tasks and locations of the role—two times—so we could get them into our bodies.

When we were finished, I looked at the job assignment schedule posted outside the zendo to see when I would have be Shoten. To my alarm, it was the next day. How could I learn the job that quickly? I always needed to rehearse a new procedure many times before I could do it properly. "Don't think. Stay in the present," I ordered myself as later I wrote out the Shoten role in my notebook. I would study it between scheduled events so I could perform it Friday evening and Saturday morning.

The first task of the Shoten comes at the end of the day. It is to ring a bell to accompany the monks as they process out of the zendo at 9 p.m. to their rooms for the night. The Shoten strikes the large, cast iron Densho bell hanging outside on the engawa, in a deep and diminishing cadence to signal the close of the day. After everyone has left the zendo, she bows to the Densho, departs the building and walks home through the dark and silent monastery. It was lovely to see everyone off to their rooms but a little spooky to walk home alone in the silent darkness.

The following morning, the Shoten has two tasks. The first is to open the monastery day shortly after 4:10 a.m. by striking a drum and a small bell on the engawa in coordination with bells being rung inside the zendo. Then to strike the Densho eighteen times over several minutes to signal the start of zazen. Following this duty the Shoten goes inside to sit three periods of zazen with the sangha. Toward the end of the third period, she listens for the sound of a match being struck some thirty feet away by a Doan-ryo monk who lights the altar candle for the morning service. The Shoten immediately leaves the zendo, goes to the drum outside, and strikes it and a small bell. Finally, the Shoten goes to the Han, also hanging outside, and in coordination with a monk down the hill outside the kitchen hitting the *Umpan* (a bronze gong rung to signal meals), she hits the Han to echo the Umpan strikes. This announces the morning service, after which oryoki breakfast is served in the zendo.

When done well, the Shoten role contributes beautifully to the opening and closing of the monastery day. For me it held particular perils. My night vision was not good. I had brought a flashlight that morning and left it on the shoe rack before entering the zendo, but I couldn't find it when I went out to do my role. The predawn morning was so dark I had to feel my way to the drum, hands out in front. I groped toward the drum but couldn't see where the drumsticks were. Fumbling to pick one up, I dropped it, making a rude clatter. Also, my hearing apparently was not acute enough to detect the cue to strike the drum. The assistant Ino rushed out to see what was wrong. I whispered an apology and completed the job as best I could. I was never again assigned to be Shoten. Exacting ceremonial roles were beyond me. I felt a moment of shame, but I was too tired to be anything but relieved to be exempt from them.

As the season slowly darkened, I realized I couldn't do much of what was expected of the monks. Perhaps I had no choice but to Just Be—in the midst of white-water action. Emanating serenity, quietude, containment, equanimity—all worthy aims of Buddhism. The next afternoon as I started down the dorm steps to go to the zendo, I did feel a warm pleasure watching the young monks dashing back for zazen, their black robes flowing behind them. Such energy and eagerness in their concentrated stride.

I continued to feel twinges of inadequacy when compared with the younger monks, but I realized my limitations were of little concern to them. Everyone was focused on their own challenges and experience. There was no way to influence them to behave in ways that would be more comfortable for me. I was free to just let others be who they were and not assume responsibility for them or for "our" relationship. Let it go. It had taken seventy-eight years of living to understand that I was not responsible for the way other people behaved.

Next day was a Personal Day. After a delicious dining room breakfast, I took a long, leisurely swim in the sunny pool. Then I got all my maintenance tasks done—clothes washed, room cleaned, yoga, bath, nap, and even a little bit of conversation with my next-door dorm mate, Yakusan. She was in her early sixties, a nurse, and a student of the Abbess. Slender and blond, she had a beautiful and ready smile. She became a supportive friend. Though the schedule allowed us only brief moments between activities, we developed shorthand communications to register our moods and offer each other support.

I finally felt more securely settled into the monastery routine. But now I became restless. I wanted something besides Zen forms and protocols to focus on. I wanted variety. I missed reading, spending a little time in someone else's mind and experience. The monastery office where we picked up our mail received the *New York Times* and *The New Yorker* magazine once a week or so, along with a few other magazines. I tried to dip into them but found I couldn't read about the world. The tone and perspectives were so alien to the silent and severely focused life at Tassajara. I couldn't make the leap back into the complexity and pain of regular life. I did investigate the small bookcase filled with paperbacks in the dormitory hallway. Itching for a little distraction, I examined the titles and found among them some good writers.

Over the next weeks I selected one book after another to enjoy during the brief breaks in the schedule. By now I had sufficiently mastered our fast pace to be able to drop in and out of it without missing a beat. I read *The Book Thief* by Markus Zusak, a young adult novel but one I found engrossing. I read *Breakfast With Buddha* by Roland Merullo, *Still Alice* by Lisa Genova, and several more. Daily I was practicing hard to stop making up stories about other people at Tassajara, but I still craved stories. The novels provided them and also brought variety and color into my monochromatic mental life, steadying me. Reading did feel a guilty pleasure—and certainly it was a practice rule during sesshins not to read or write. But surely these books wouldn't be in our bookcase if they were not permitted. . .? I decided I didn't need to know the answer to that question.

Chapter Twelve

Sangha Encounters

One evening early in November, following the final period of evening zazen, I had a brief, nasty encounter with my unfriendly seatmate, whom I will call Sherry. Earlier that evening, one of the Doan-ryo monks left a small note on the zabuton of my other seatmate, whom I will call Barb. Notes were the way the practice leadership reminded a monk that he/she had a particular job the next day. That evening Sherry had sat in Barb's seat for dinner because Barb was away that day. (Monks were served in twos by the servers, who couldn't easily get to monks in corner seats, such as Sherry's, so she had to move to another seat for that meal.)

I thought the note on Barb's mat had information she might need before the next morning. I thought it would be helpful if I took it back to the dorm, where she lived across the hall from me. So at 9:00 p.m. as we stood waiting to file out of the zendo, I picked up the note. Seeing me do this, Sherry punctiliously snatched it from my hand and placed it back on Barb's cushion. I whispered that I wanted to take it to Barb, but Sherry sniffed and brushed past me to exit the zendo.

I felt humiliated and then immediately outraged at being so categorically dismissed. When I got back to the dorm, I wrote a note to Barb that I taped to her door, telling her about what Sherry had done with the note on her cushion. When Barb returned, she came to my room and sternly chastised me. "You shouldn't have taken the note. It was none of your business."

I was mortified. Shocked into a dead sleep.

Next morning, I awoke still upset, furious, in fact. Silently I wished harm to Sherry for her imperious behavior. I knew the rage I felt was inappropriate and would come back around to bite me, but I couldn't control it. I was grateful we lived in silence. It would have been far worse if I had expressed my anger—to anyone. The leopard from my dream a week earlier came to mind. The rage I was feeling now had the power of that leopard: unexpected, ferocious.

Why did Sherry's dismissal feel so threatening? I felt humiliated, shamed. Scenes from the past flashed through me: being bullied in eighth grade; years later repeatedly intimidated by my inebriated spouse. Recalling those painful episodes, I felt rage rise in my chest and throat. I was shocked. Was this the dream leopard? Had I suppressed it all these years? Was the leopard not my enemy but my defender? Had these weeks of zazen and living in silence at Tassajara finally allowed me access to my deeper mind? My power?

I was exhausted by this emotional tumult. I didn't want to talk with anyone. I needed to recover some mental balance. As I silently followed the day's schedule, I realized that actually it had not been my place to take Barb's note. The shock of Sherry's dismissal and the strong reaction I had to it made me see now how blindly I had behaved. I had not actually been thinking. Perhaps I was lost in the dream of zazen. Being jarred out of the spaciousness of zazen could arouse unexpected, even inexplicable, emotions. Rage rarely erupts openly because meditators normally do not interfere with each other. But the intensity of zazen can generate strong emotions and even actions.

As I reflected further, I recognized how liberating (if painful) it was to be smacked into awareness in this way—like a heart defibrillator applied to the mind. I had long been grateful to Zen teachers and friends, coming out of the power of zazen, for holding up a mirror for me to see myself from the outside and shock me into accurate self-awareness. I rarely got this "assistance" from social friends. Ajahn Chah's advice about letting go of unwholesome thoughts came to mind again: I needed to focus on myself, mind my own business. I vowed to try, but I found it hard to stop thinking about Sherry's behavior. Her evident contempt stung.

That afternoon, during work period I sewed part of a silk rakusu, a sangha gift for the Shuso at a ceremony at the end of practice period. I had volunteered to do this, and it was soothing work. My bodily energy was low. It seemed that other people also felt low. The woman across the hall from me had slept for the past two days, not coming to the zendo at all. The Abbess told us she herself would take the evening off.

In the quiet work of hand sewing, I continued to reflect on the anger I felt. Now a full day after the event, I realized that the rage might be due to having my strategy to gain acceptance, being helpful, called into question. Did I so depend on this device that when I was prevented from using it, I felt existentially threatened? Was my self-identity so fragile that it must be this radically protected? In earlier weeks of practice period I had come to see that always trying to be helpful could be manipulative, and I had begun to relax around it. Now I could see that this Habit Body was so deeply embedded that my impulse to take the note to Barb was reflexive, without conscious decision. It was Sherry's impatient reaction that exposed my dependence on the Karma Body habit. A few days passed. I calmed down and didn't feel so much at threat. I was grateful for the insights the episode offered.

On the next Work Day I was assigned to clean the Student Refrigerator, a full-sized cooler located outside the dining room building. Monks with special diets kept their concoctions there for times when oryoki food contained ingredients they couldn't eat. I found it full of mostly decomposing food in plastic containers, which I either threw out or left notes asking their owners to dispose of them. I removed all the shelves and scrubbed them in the small outdoor sink in the coffee area across the commons area. The job took the full three hours of morning work period, a lot of labor but satisfying, especially in that it appeared it hadn't been done for perhaps a year. Later, the Work Leader reported that the Tanto was amazed at its transformation. I especially enjoyed this news—both because the Tanto seemed to be pretty hard to impress and because it was kind of the Work Leader to tell me. I felt a little more a part of Tassajara.

According to conventional wisdom, it takes three months to change or establish a habit. It might have been a happy coincidence for me that practice period was for three months. I longed for mental transformation. I wanted to be rid of the self-centeredness and strong preferences I was observing in myself. These might be loosening now, having less purchase, but I wasn't sure. The recent episode of rage to the contrary, I did seem to let go of lesser annoyances more readily. Also more manageable, strong emotions were being stirred up, and I was having useful insights into my early conditioning. What I wanted was more time to integrate the experiences I was having. Normally, integration time greatly enriched almost everything I did—traveling, reading, talking with friends, Zen retreats. I got as much from reflection afterward as I did from the experience itself. But here the schedule pushed us on to the next activity and the next before I could integrate much of anything.

I had become aware that I was not having any joyful or blissful moments in zazen, as usually occurred in prolonged sitting. I seemed to be engaged in a continual struggle, both on and off the cushion, just to keep going and be on time. I was troubled by the absence of any spiritual feelings of oneness or connection with others that I usually experienced, especially during sesshins. Rather than feeling related to those around me, my focus was either on observing my reactions to what I was doing or on bodily sensations: in the zendo sitting up straight in zazen, easing a sore knee; outside feeling and hearing my own footfalls on the silty pathway to the Baths; standing docilely in Work Circle waiting for the next thing and the next; at night feeling blissful relief when at last I lay down to sleep. Was I directly experiencing reality instead of shaping it by my preferences and interpretations? This was the aim of Zen. Could my accumulating exhaustion ironically be the vehicle for reaching the present moment?

I reflected intermittently on the blunt encounter with Sherry. I wanted to understand the strong reaction I had. I recalled originally feeling sorry for her when early in practice period we Tangaryo students were required to explain to the assembled monks how and why we came to Zen. Sherry spoke about a difficult childhood, including abandonment by a parent. She was from the same part of California where I had lived. Feeling that connection and wanting to support her, after her talk I had made a point to thank her. Thereafter I tried to communicate sympathy to her nonverbally by smiling when we passed on the pathway. She might have been put off by my old age or maybe even felt I was patronizing her. I was frustrated that she never responded and then later, of course, shocked and alienated when she reprimanded me. Now that I had uncovered my motive for being helpful to others as a way to be accepted, I could see these attempts at befriending her might have annoyed her. She might have intuited and felt pressured by my unconscious neediness and so withheld herself, inside the zendo and out.

On the next Work Day, when the monks could speak briefly with each other, Barb told me Sherry said she didn't like sitting next to me because I was too slow getting on and off my cushion. Barb suggested I switch places with Sherry. My initial reaction was to feel at fault and agree to this change, but on consideration, I realized this was just old conditioning reacting. If I sat in the corner where Sherry did, I would have to move to different seats for oryoki meals. I'd have to take several support cushions with me, plus my "great" slowness would then bother several additional people. I chafed at Barb's effort to manipulate me, but I decided to wait to see if she or Sherry pushed more. This proposal did not come up again, and I congratulated myself on withstanding Barb's pressure. A small victory, but given the nature of the early conditioning I was discovering, an encouraging one.

That evening at Tassajara, the Director gave a good talk on sangha practice. She quoted from the koan, Dizan's Nearness, the line, "Not knowing is most intimate" (or nearest). Not knowing, she told us, means not grabbing or holding on to our idea of what's happening. This was a useful teaching for sangha relationships because we actually don't know the causes and conditions of another person's behavior. Lacking that information, we make up stories to explain their behavior, and then we base our own behavior on our stories. Thus we limit our understanding of the other person, possibly even misunderstanding them altogether.

Referring to the Abbess's earlier teaching about making up stories, the Director asked why we create stories about other people. And why do our stories become *fixed views*? The mind behaves this way a lot—sometimes for entertainment and sometimes because, as social animals, we want or need to "figure out" what motivates people so we can relate to them (or in my case feel safe in their presence). We look for differences; we discriminate among things we encounter. This is a primitive survival mechanism. We need to distinguish a stick on the ground from a poisonous snake. The trouble is that the conscious mind doesn't know when to quit discriminating. Also because our stories are never current with reality (which is always changing), they can be misleading, even dangerous. To help us let go of our stories, we must practice generosity, the Director said. We must give people the benefit of the doubt, instead of interpreting their actions to fit our past story about them.

Buddhism teaches us to be open to what is—not to what we think is—so we can respond appropriately. The problem is our expectations (stories) affect and even limit the other person's behavior. When we let go of our stories, we free the other person to change. But given that we always seem to bring our archetypes with us into new situations, how can we arrive at "Don't know"? We must notice that when we find fault with someone, we are projecting onto them something about our self we do not like. We make up a story based on unconscious biases—like the time I believed I was being helpful to Barb by taking a note to her, when my actual motive was more likely to gain her appreciation and acceptance.

The Director's talk reinforced what I had begun to notice and respond to in my relationships with others at Tassajara. I was having some success at letting go of my stories about other individuals. When I realized I was being judgmental, I practiced, "Don't know" and found it a great relief to come back into a more neutral mental balance. It was freeing not to have to react or to know anything. I didn't need stories. Without them I felt closer to the truth. And less alone. Curiously, trying to understand someone else separates us because we objectify the other person in order to analyze him.

I also saw how I could apply this teaching to the "story" I had about myself. At Tassajara, I was reduced to just this present body/mind. Others did not know my history or biography or resume. I was just what I appeared to be. Some saw an old woman and were perhaps repelled or afraid, depending on their stories. Others saw just another monk, different from most, but acceptable. My story wasn't important or apparent. This anonymity was both uncomfortable and liberating. I had no standing based on past accomplishments, but I was freed from the political and social struggle that comes with having a self-manufactured identity. It could feel lonely, but it was also a relief not to have a history. I considered the fixed views I had brought to Tassajara and how they could be abandoned. To confirm this progress, in my Dharma Notebook I made a list of the stories I could do without:

- *Needing full information before agreeing to do something is essential.* At Tassajara little information was provided. I had adjusted to living and acting without detailed guidance.
- *If I didn't know what was happening in the world, I could not be the responsible citizen I wanted to be.* Isolated as I was here at Tassajara,

however, I had to admit that the world continued to turn without my help or even my attention.

- *Having a pleasant appearance was essential to survival. Otherwise I might offend others and be rejected.* I had always believed that I was ugly because of my back, and I compensated accordingly. Now, for the first time as an adult, I wore no makeup and was generally grungy. My appearance was no worse than anyone else's at Tassajara. But other people did not appear to reject me. Dropping this habitual, anxious self consciousness was liberating.
- *It was essential always to help others and never need or ask for their help.* Here I found I could allow others to help me, and needed to do so—a major step in growing old.
- *As a priest, I must know and do all the practice forms correctly; otherwise I would fail.* Even though I couldn't receive all the training here, I believed that over time I would be able to find my way as a priest—which involved much more than knowing the forms.
- *Knowing is essential, critical.* Actually, not knowing is more important.

We were nearing the third month of practice period. I seemed to have gotten my bearings. Now, for the first time, I could turn away from the urgent focus on learning the monastic requirements. I could observe the community at large, its mood and tone, its culture. I began to see signs of a complex and intense social life playing out behind the scrim of our monastic silence. One day a young woman suddenly moved into our dorm, which had been designated for women over age fifty-five who might need heat in cold weather. No introduction or explanation was offered, and in our silence, we did not ask. I wondered about her only as she passed listlessly in the dorm hallway, obviously unhappy. Some weeks later, I learned that her boyfriend, another resident monk, had broken up with her, and she'd had to move out of their cabin.

One night as I was returning to the dorm at 9 p.m. following evening zazen, the same young woman emerged, carrying a large baking tray full of aromatic, puffy sweet rolls. In response to the surprise on my face, she whispered the rolls were for a party she was going to later. They had been rising in her warm room through the evening and were now ready to be baked in the kitchen oven. Next day another monk revealed there was a lively after-hours social scene going on. Ah, the silence we kept contained much more than self-reflection.

In fact I had begun to sense a fair amount of relational intensity and sexual energy in the community, as one would expect in a group of young people living together—straight, gay, and trans. I felt this energy more in the zendo than outside at other gatherings where the monks had more space to interact with each other. The intensity of zazen could heighten emotions. When I lived at Sogenji in Japan twenty years earlier, I heard about the crushes some of the young women monks had on some of the men monks and even about a few forbidden assignations. Here at Tassajara from time to time I observed longing looks cast across the zendo at other monks, some of whom appeared oblivious to their admirers. I recalled the poignancy I too had experienced when young and in love with the wrong fellow.

Then one morning, during oryoki breakfast I thought I might be witnessing a secret love affair being quietly conducted in our midst between a female food server and a male monk. The server sneaked looks at the monk while she was coming and going in the zendo. He grinned briefly in return and quickly looked down. I felt idiotic to be "spying" on some else's love life—in the zendo, yet—but this little *pas de deux* felt sweet. I was as amused by the interest I felt in someone else's sex life—and at my advanced age—as I was by the episode itself. Soon enough, breakfast concluded, we all returned to our solitary silence—I, refreshed from this secret interlude. It could be that my mind had made up the story entirely, though I don't think so. . . .

Soon after, I became aware of another aspect of community life. I sensed some ambivalence about the Abbess's admonitions to us to be considerate of each other. On one occasion she remonstrated with us, quite kindly, I thought, to keep the outdoor coffee and tea area neat. The area had a sink with hot water and sponges and paper towels for washing up, but it was usually messy. I was amused that the Abbess needed to instruct us that part of living in sangha was cleaning up after ourselves so that the next person didn't deal with an unhealthy food area. I appreciated that the majority of the sangha were young men and women who might never have had to concern themselves with keeping a kitchen area clean. They needed training. Another time the Abbess asked us all to be more mindful as we departed the zendo. She requested that when we took our shoes from the shoe shelves, we not drop them noisily onto the wooden engawa and then shuffle audibly down the pebbled stairway. The noise disturbed the monks in zazen.

I appreciated the Abbess's reminders and the care with which she delivered them. I sensed, however, a bit of squirming at these lessons in decorum. Were these just "bad boys" resisting being told what to do by a "mother" figure? To me, the Abbess was a highly qualified and deeply compassionate leader, but the Zen Buddhist monastic tradition still exuded the masculine dominance of its origins. And men and women do lead differently.

A few evenings later during a community program in the dining room, we were asked to break into small groups to discuss what we were learning about living in community, the practice period theme. After that, we would share our insights with the entire group. The Abbess had designed the meeting format, a proven, effective way to stimulate group participation. However, at the last minute she was called away and could not lead it. In her absence, it turned out that some monks refused to discuss this topic. In the group of five I was in, only three of us were willing to speak. In one or two other groups, I heard afterward, no one at all spoke. Out in the "civilian" world, this would have clearly indicated passive resistance to—something— in this case, exactly what, I didn't know. Was there a festering conflict I knew nothing about?

At around this time, one resident monk appeared to have sunk into a deep depression. Out of the zendo he drifted around morosely, no longer making eye contact. I became alarmed about his condition, fearing he might try to harm himself. Finally, with apologies for intruding, I asked the Abbess if anyone was working with him. She told me, Yes, someone was. I was relieved to know this and would have liked to know more but felt I couldn't ask about it further. It might invade his privacy. Whatever the case, I definitely felt dismay and unsettledness in the community. Even I, excused for health reasons from working and interacting on a serving crew, couldn't live this closely with others without picking up some unspoken feelings. Misunderstandings, interpersonal miseries, and political rivalries could be pushed out of sight, but they did not go away. They festered. It was distressing to witness unhealthy dynamics, and have no way to help. My old Karma Body rising again.

Chapter Thirteen

Rope's End

In mid-November we entered the final month of practice period. The days were still warm, eighty degrees by noon, but near freezing at 4:00 a.m. I had the monastery routine down well enough to believe that if I just kept trying, I could make it to the end. We had two more seven-day sesshins to sit. The momentum toward ever deeper practice was building. The expectation was that all of us monks would attempt to break through our conditioning. Head down, I would go forward.

My body/mind had another plan. Two months of sleep deprivation seemed to be as long as I could hang onto the rope of my determination. The mind now flipped chaotically in all directions—from determination to resentment, anxiety to anger, resignation to hope, blame to gratitude, appreciation to despair. I couldn't modulate the intensity of my thoughts and feelings, let alone direct them. They sank and soared on their own. Repeatedly, when I vowed to get more sleep, I continued to sit zazen every evening. Repeatedly, when I resented someone's behavior and I applied the antidote Don't Know, soon I fell back into blaming. The cognitive brain was no longer in charge. The mind was running its own crazy relay race but repeatedly dropping the baton. Sometimes I slept well at night but the next day was so exhausted I could barely move. Other times I slept poorly but felt energetic next morning. When I was not tossed around by gusts of emotions, I seemed adrift mentally, increasingly missing connections between events. Was I finally living in the moment? Or was I unraveling?

Midway into the penultimate seven-day sesshin, I took offense at the morning's dharma talk given by the Tanto. He said that practice period was about work, not about philosophy (or something like that; I wasn't clear). He seemed to be scolding us. Was he being sarcastic or patronizing? I was confused. The schedule was hard enough. I didn't need any more pressure.

After the talk, sitting zazen outside, I puzzled over my irritation. I couldn't tie it to anything specific in the dharma talk. In fact, I couldn't remember what the talk was about. Maybe my mind was slipping. I realized I no longer remembered the dharma talks, which up to then I had been able to summarize afterward in my Dharma Notebook.

I grew stiff sitting outside. I looked around to see what the other monks were doing, but I didn't see anyone else about. I should have returned to the zendo, but I went instead to the dorm. As I lay on my bed waiting for the next period of zazen, I heard two small planes flying low overhead. Were they fire planes? In the continuing severe drought, a fire could start at the slightest spark. I hoped a forest fire wasn't what all this hardship was leading to.

As I continued to rest, I drifted mentally. Suddenly I saw a connection between the annoyance I felt at the Tanto's talk and the anxiety I had about fire. Could I trust the Tanto to keep the community safe? The question startled me. I realized I was conflating two quite separate things. His judgment might be reliable when it came to fire safety, and I might still disagree with something he said. Was I just looking for someone to blame for my misery? How devious the mind can be. I was a little uncomfortable with the Tanto, but I appreciated what I was learning about myself from our sometimes bumpy encounters.

On another sesshin day, in her dharma talk the Abbess returned to the theme of the Habit Body and letting things be what they are. Not interpreting, not allowing previous experience and judgments to distort current perceptions. Even though we think we know what will happen, she said, we actually don't know. Believing that we do know, we create repetitive experiences. What an insight! I thought. We habitually shape our response to new experiences based on previous experiences. This limits our new experiences, at least partially, to our past experiences. When I blame someone for something I don't like, I should be suspicious, not satisfied. I might be distorting the present by assuming it is like the past. I should just drop the judgment. Let the new experience speak for itself.

The Abbess's talk energized me. In the late afternoon, zazen was refreshingly productive. The conflict with Sherry arose in my mind, but instead of whining about being unfairly treated, I pushed down into the misery I felt. A question arose, "Why is it so hard to accept being rejected?" Remembering the Director's advice to be curious about negative feelings, I observed my body. My stomach felt knotted, tight: anger. My heart and throat felt constricted: fear of rejection, not having a right to be myself. Behind my eyes, tears were welling: rejection, hurt, loneliness. I breathed with these feelings for a few minutes.

I recalled other times when I'd felt rejected for reasons I didn't understand, and suddenly I knew I could respond differently now. Instead of resisting rejection, I could work with it just as it was. As the Abbess recommended, I could meet the experience, not add to it the residue of past experience. I asked myself, "What would it take to accept Sherry's rejection?"

Immediately a new question arose: "What might *she* be feeling that caused her to push me away so categorically?" I mused for a few minutes on this question but found no logical explanation. Instead I *felt* she couldn't speak, couldn't communicate, as if someone or something muted her. I explored this. I wondered what it felt like to be Sherry. Immediately I felt suffocated, as perhaps she did. I felt like *I* couldn't speak. Then I experienced a sudden rush of energy. I was my former self again: awake, energetic, and interested in this problem. No more feeling stuck. No more blaming and projecting. Letting Sherry somatically into my consciousness released the anguish I had been holding for over two months.

The wonder of zazen: when we wrest our attention away from self-centered cravings and accept others just as they are, we allow them and our relationships oxygen. Then everyone can breathe freely. This was Thich Nhat Hanh's concept of Inter-being: We co-create each other. We're all, by nature, intimately interrelated.

Another sesshin day, another challenge. That evening the Tanto scolded me. I was in my pajamas ready to crawl into bed when he came to my dorm room, knocked on the door and stepped in. Smiling pleasantly, he said, "I noticed you taking notes during the Abbess's talk. Note taking is not allowed in the zendo."

"I've tried just listening, but lately I can't remember anything afterward," I explained.

"Note taking is not allowed in the zendo," he repeated.

As a long-time Zen student, I understood the tradition that monks must do as directed. We were expected to follow instructions for performing a practice role and to graciously accept critical feedback for any mistakes made. "Of course," I replied. "I will obey the rule."

Being chastised at bedtime shook me a little, but I recalled that the Buddha did not develop monastic rules until he learned of a mistake. Only then would he create a rule to help the sangha maintain harmony. (The original rules eventually grew to 227 for male monks and 331 for nuns—!) The Tanto was discharging his disciplinary responsibility to maintain harmony in the sangha, and I was responding with a monk's humility.

Next morning I still felt in jeopardy, but the Abiding Lay Teacher saved me. She gave a simple, pithy dharma talk on the value of intimacy with others. She noted that change is continuous. Internal and external influences impact us. Responding or not responding changes the initial situation and also changes us. We become the next version of ourselves based on our interactions with others. This process is subtle. In our interactions with others, old habits are activated. We should study them. Release our old habits or realize we need to study them more to better understand reality. Zazen is about meeting these aspects of ourselves, observing them, letting go of them; seeing that they make us suffer; realizing that they make others suffer too. She said, Remember Don't Know mind. Use it.

On the last day of sesshin in the early morning I felt clear-headed, energetic, hopeful, even happy. But after an 8 a.m. nap, I was exhausted again, almost sick. My skin felt sensitive, my brain frazzled. It took such effort to keep focused and do the next thing and the next. I wished someone would take care of me. But there was no one. I recalled a line from a beautiful sutra we sometimes chanted about "saving the body." This would become my mantra: I must save myself.

Next day on Regular Schedule, I worried about my mood swings during sesshin. My mind might be letting go of habitual patterns, but it felt precarious. On the last day of sesshin I had heard footsteps I'd never heard before outside the zendo on the engawa. Panic rose in my throat as I imagined marauders sneaking up on us. After several minutes of pitched anxiety, I realized it must be the lunch servers bringing our meal. I relaxed. As it turned out, it was the sesshin cooks assembling for their jundo, the ceremonial walk in the zendo so the monks could thank them for feeding us. Before my frenzied mind realized the cause of those sounds, I had felt physically threatened.

That afternoon my skin felt sore, feverish. My senses were raw, as if I would explode if anyone touched or opposed me. I decided not to sit the next periods of zazen. I signed out on the Tenken Sheet and stayed in the dorm, though I was unable to sleep or do anything but lie on the bed and look out the window. I felt as if I were disintegrating. Helpless, without any capacity to defend myself. Finally I got up and did some yoga in the small floor space of the room. This helped regain a small sense of agency. Maybe I could still affect what I was experiencing. I knew a mental breakdown—which was what seemed to be happening—could be a good thing because it might catalyze a breakthrough in understanding. The Abbess had suggested my mind could be letting go of the Karma Body a little bit at a time. Instead of being gradual, the process was more a series of jerks and jolts. Maybe I should try to relax and let it be.

Thanksgiving Day came. It happened to be a Work Day, so we worked at our assigned jobs until 1:00 p.m. Then we celebrated with a banquet in the dining room. The Tenzo and kitchen crew had worked all morning and much of the previous day to prepare nut loaf and mashed potatoes with mushroom gravy; bright green, parboiled string beans; a jellied salad; fresh baked rolls with butter; and a delicious ice cream cake dessert. The Doan-ryo members set up and decorated the dining room. We monks could sit anywhere we wanted, eat as much as we could hold, and talk to whomever we were near. A true celebration: having choices.

The pleasures of Thanksgiving Day led me to reflect on how odd it was to be so deeply removed from regular life. A few residents drove out from the monastery each week to transact business, buy supplies and collect the mail, but most of us never left the monastery, and in this last month I had begun to feel the isolation. I did hear occasional jets flying high above, so I knew Western "civilization" continued, though entirely without my influence. I began to wonder if I existed in any practical way. Had my efforts at political persuasion over the years been of any use—or even substance? Now that I had no impact at all, I wondered if the impact I had hoped to have had been a fiction.

How perilous it felt to live so far out of the stream of life. I believed I was protected by the monastic institution, but being so remote and lacking news from the world, I felt vulnerable. Having no close friends within the community also probably added to my sense of vulnerability. I might easily be overlooked or forgotten, despite the Tenken's daily "seat-checking."

No one was mistreating me at Tassajara, but I wasn't thriving. I was barely keeping up. The Buddha taught us to rely on our own experience to decide what is right for us. In more normal circumstances I had been able to do this, but now on my last leg, I couldn't find the inner resources to be strong. The life perspective I had developed in childhood was that other people, especially in groups, might at any time turn on me, so I'd better be prepared. I would avoid perilous situations, but if unavoidable, I would withdraw, go inward—perhaps calling on my then hidden leopard energy for self-protection.

As I matured and grew in life experience, I refined this dour perspective. I researched activities I was drawn to before I committed to doing them so that I had a reasonable expectation of success. I developed strategies for challenges I could foresee (such as managing pain during Tangaryo by changing zazen positions). I developed a repertoire of caution, skill, and avoidance to cope with rejection from others. These strategies masked a hidden but fierce determination to succeed—and attracted me to Zen. Now that my inner leopard had surfaced, I might consciously draw on its energy to complete practice period.

That evening in the dining room, the Abbess conducted an excellent class on practicing in community, a topic pertinent to my recent feelings of isolation. I could take notes because this was a lecture, not a dharma talk in the zendo. The Abbess asked us to focus for the remainder of practice period on how we practiced as a sangha. Her theme was how sangha practice supports individual practice. In sangha life, she told us, inclusiveness is important. We need to be able to love and include everyone equally. The Bodhisattva way is to accept all aspects of everyone and of ourselves too. We can support each other even by the way we move with and around each other in our daily activities—with awareness and respect (such a lovely idea, I thought). We should also regard each other as teachers who reveal to us our preferences and how our desires limit our experience.

As we live together, emotions often cause us trouble, the Abbess continued. Emotions are unpredictable. They simply arise. Emotions reside in the primitive limbic brain and come into our awareness directly, not going through the cerebral cortex where they can be processed rationally. Emotions like anger or fear are somatic experiences, not cognitive experiences. Initially, emotions are out of our control. But we *can* control how we act in response to them. Once we are aware of an emotion, we can rationally determine our thoughts and actions. Because our thoughts, speech, and actions can strongly affect others, the Abbess said, it is critical that we pay attention to our emotions before we act or react.

When we identify with a strong emotion, we create a problem. We want to hold onto what we like and push away what we don't like. But there's a solution: Meditation practice develops the capacity to simply acknowledge and hold emotions and then release them without acting on them. In fact, the less we meddle in an emotion, the faster it subsides. We don't have to do anything with our emotion but observe it with kindness and patience. This helps it lose its power. We must cultivate an unconditional capacity to meet and let things be as they are, rather than emotionally coloring them with our preconceived beliefs or story.

The Abbess pointed out specific mistakes people in community commonly make: When we fantasize about people, we treat them as objects for our entertainment. When we act as a self-appointed teacher or boss of others, we violate their psychological boundaries. When we make assumptions about others to help us feel in control, we end up feeling separate, not interrelated. When we realize we are making up a story about someone, we must stop. Instead, become interested in *why* we think this story must be told. Then let go of it. It takes courage to look at and accept ourselves, the Abbess acknowledged, but this is the opportunity of sangha life.

With just three weeks of practice period remaining, I began to daydream about home: imagining my house and garden, seeing friends, returning to Red Cedar zendo, driving, riding the bus again. I was dismayed to find that this fantasizing only led to impatience and ennui. To dispel my restlessness, I wrote a list of things I was grateful for at Tassajara and posted it on my wall: Good health (I wasn't sick in bed), agility (I was doing yoga daily to preserve strength and flexibility), loss of weight but no hunger pangs, some friendly faces among the Tassajara sangha, support from my sons and friends back home who wrote often, the beauty of Tassajara, the beauty and meaning of the sutra chants, discovering the mind, abandoning bad mental habits, the accommodations made so I could rest and do work I could manage, and my long years of Zen practice that made it possible to keep going here. Good reminders.

In these final weeks the Abbess continued to focus on practicing in sangha. She spoke about conflict, saying a conflict between two or more people is usually complex. It arises from the immediately preceding circumstances of each person, as well as from their historical experiences. When we have a conflict with someone, it is pointless to blame the other party because we can't change anyone else. We should focus on ourselves. Ask, "What in me participates in this conflict? What practice will help me?" Acknowledge what we contribute to the conflict. The Abbess advised us to muse on the classical Buddhist teaching about the ephemerality of life, the Five Remembrances, which remind us that we will grow old, become ill, change, and ultimately die. This helps to put conflicts in perspective.

The teaching of Right Speech is also important for sangha wellbeing. Wrong speech includes lying, slandering, criticizing, gossiping, and speaking carelessly or profanely. When we violate Right Speech in one of these ways, we disturb or prevent our "meeting" others. We also violate Right Speech when we tell a secret about someone to a third party—or agree to hear and keep a secret about someone else. Secrets impair relationships with the person being talked about, and they burden third parties by involving them involuntarily in our problem.

We can also violate Right Speech when we praise ourselves in comparison to another. When we elevate ourselves or dwell on others' faults in order to feel good about ourselves, we implicitly diminish others. When we ask a third party to intervene on our behalf with another person, we violate Right Speech. If we have a problem with someone that we are unable to resolve, we should go to a practice leader, not to complain but to explore what we ourselves are contributing to the problem. I was pleased to realize I had done this when I had the opportunity to speak with the Abiding Teacher about the struggle with Sherry. I'm sure this helped loosen my anger so that later it finally dissolved in the mental spaciousness of zazen.

The Abbess concluded her recommendations on Right Speech as essential to sangha life with the following definition: "Right Speech is speech at the right time, in truth, with affection, and beneficial with the mind of good will toward all." Before you speak, she said, ask yourself, "Does what I have to say meet all these criteria?" If not, don't speak. When someone asks you for feedback, the Abbess advised, first think carefully. Simmer on what you want to say until you can give the feedback in a nonjudgmental, non-harming way. Perhaps you will find the words, or perhaps you won't say anything.

I was grateful for the Abbess's wise teachings about relationships. They were balm to my otherwise unpleasantly mercurial states of mind. On cue, next morning the sense of satisfaction I felt had shifted dramatically. Perhaps it was because it was oppressively warm for early December. I felt heavily depressed, more so than I'd ever felt in my life. The wide swings of emotion I was experiencing now were alarming—deadening ennui followed by sharp anxiety. If these days were to be my last ones, I didn't want to live them this way. I was grateful to be excused from the rigorous practice period roles the other Tangaryo students continued to fill. But an unexpected consequence was that I had little interaction with others, not even the dubious stimulation of a conflict over work. Lack of interaction for three months had left me desolate.

I had always been resourceful at diverting myself, but now I was too bone tired to think creatively about how to stay engaged. In Japan twenty years earlier, my activities were more diverse, but during the final two months there, I suffered the tedium and restrictions of living in a culture I didn't understand. Now at Tassajara, another culture I sometimes found difficult, I was shocked to be in a black depression. Finally, in the late afternoon, a few minutes with my next-door dorm-mate describing my misery pulled me out of it. How much we depend on each other. I ended the day with a new respect and sympathy for those who suffer clinical depression—my husband Dave, to name one. Just a taste of it had felt devastating. Years of heavy hopelessness had led him to end his life.

Chapter Fourteen

Save the Body

My unraveling continued. Early mornings in December, the temperature was 20 degrees F. At a work meeting, the Director announced a disturbing new detail about our departure from Tassajara, which would take place a few days after Rohatsu sesshin. Since every minute of sesshin was scheduled, there would be no time allotted to packing. We must organize our belongings between sesshin events and have our luggage to the truck by 3:30 p.m. the day before departure. We should keep our bedding until the final day and must not pack the robes we would wear in the closing ceremony. We would have to shove these sacred garments into our backpacks along with our oryoki bowls just before leaving. In disbelief, we worn out Tangaryo monks grimaced and exchanged eye rolls. I did appreciate that the Director prefaced her announcement by admitting she hated to have to tell us this. I was grateful for that small gesture of empathy.

The next day I almost lost it—twice—in the zendo. During morning service, Barb, who was kneeling behind me, became impatient waiting for me to pass the chant books back. I was struggling to stand up, but my hand had caught in the long sleeve of my koromo, and I couldn't pass the books quickly. She slapped my bare toes protruding from under my robes. At evening service, again she was upset that I was too slow. She glared and almost grabbed the books away from me. I hissed, "Stop being so impatient! I'm going as fast as I can!" my anger noted with amusement by nearby monks. After the service when I simmered down, I realized I had finally hit the wall. When we left the zendo for the night, I asked the Abbess's Jisha if I could have an emergency dokusan. I was falling apart and needed help. Actually what I said was, "I'm afraid I'm going to punch Barb." This was a ludicrous threat, given that Barb was twice as strong as I was, not to speak of our Buddhist vow to do no harm. The Jisha and I chuckled together briefly over this absurdity, but I explained I needed help as soon as possible, though of course the next morning would be okay if the Abbess was too tired that evening.

A few minutes later, the Abbess came to my room. I was already dressed for bed. "I'm feeling panicky," I told her. "I think I must leave Tassajara. I'm afraid I won't get enough rest during Rohatsu." As the re-enactment of the Buddha's enlightenment, Rohatsu is the year's culminating sesshin, the time for great effort and great promise. After these months of struggle and persistence, I was hoping to experience a breakthrough in understanding.

"Don't worry," the Abbess said. "Take it one day at a time. Tomorrow morning, don't get up for early zazen. Wait and come to breakfast in the zendo, and then later talk with me again to see what you should do next."

I was touched that the Abbess had made the effort to come see me and grateful for her advice. I slept pretty well, but of course I woke, as on every other day, to the clanging of the wake-up bell. I remained in bed, planning to sleep another hour before getting up. But I started thinking about how to get through the rest of practice period, and I couldn't relax. After a few minutes I realized I was feeling panicky, as if I was suffocating. I thought about the relentless, repetitive, confining schedule of events that was our daily life. The weight of it had become unendurable.

It occurred to me that I was having a panic attack. I'd never experienced one, though years before I had helped a friend through hers by holding her hand and walking with her. Now to escape my agitation, I got up and dressed. When my dorm friend Yakusan returned on the brief break after oryoki breakfast, I told her how I felt. She'd had panic attacks and recognized the symptoms. She said to drink lots of water and just watch the episodes when they occurred. They subside pretty quickly once you realize what is happening. I was grateful for her sympathy and advice. I was so worn down that I didn't know where to turn.

It was cold as Rohatsu got under way. I wore several layers of clothing in the zendo, where the heat was not working well. It was also cold in the dorm. I napped from 8:00 to 9:30 a.m., although I had planned on sleeping no more than an hour. It was solid sleep and I was slow to wake. When I returned to the zendo, I was alarmed to see everyone standing outside. What had happened? My heart pounded. Had Abbot Steve died? It turned out that because the zendo was cold, the monks were going to take a brisk walk to warm up. The Shuso led everyone down the entire compound and back. Returning to the still cold zendo, to keep warm, we were instructed to do fifteen minutes of full prostration bows prior to each meal.

In zazen I found myself worrying that terrible things might be happening in the world. It felt eerie not to know what was going on outside our deep, isolated valley. Like being dead. Rationally, I knew the world went on without my awareness and input, but it scared me to be so out of touch. In the final minutes of morning zazen, panic clutched my throat. I couldn't get enough air. I realized it must be my ego self that felt threatened. I understood the teaching that "I"—a separate, ongoing entity—did not exist. There was only this and this and this, moment by moment. "This" for me was Tassajara—trees, rocks, deer, sky, cold air, zendo, monks, oryoki, and eventually sleep. But I didn't want to be there for "this" anymore. I felt trapped. I panicked.

My mind was so unruly, turbulent, and obstinate. Why couldn't it accept what was? Why did it cling to what wasn't? What it couldn't have? I was so uncomfortable: grinding stomach, shortness of breath, resistance, resistance. I didn't know what to do except endure it, like a convalescent whose progress is agonizingly slow. How to live through these final days? The teaching was just to face it all, but I was hating Zen right then. I didn't want to struggle this hard. I wanted uplifting talks about oneness and compassion, not this ragged, brutal confrontation with the "self." Could struggling this hard be good? Maybe I was too old, my mind too entrenched, brain cells unable to release their habitual patterns. But what was the alternative? Stop trying? Fake it? The idea repulsed me.

I would have to ride out these final days in whatever way I could. I wondered if my earlier watchword, *Just Being*, included Being Broken.

There were just two weeks until the end of practice period. Despite Rohatsu's promise of breakthrough, I decided to sign out for evening zazen. I knew it was important to follow the schedule completely, but I was too crazy to be around anyone. I was desperate to finish practice period—just a few more days to go—but I didn't know if I could. Sleep seemed the only medicine for the relentless pressure I was experiencing.

Rohatsu proceeded day by day. Wearing seven layers of clothing kept me almost warm in the zendo. I worked in two naps a day. I dealt with my chaotic mind as best I could, knowing the turbulence was of my own making. Then one morning the Abbess started her dharma talk by saying she felt a sense of dread. She wished she could cancel the sesshin, but of course she would not. This got everyone's attention. Murmurs of dismay rippled throughout the zendo. I was alarmed. Had my mental turmoil been a response to some impending doom that she too had intuited? Then remembering I was not the center of the universe, I felt concern for her. Poor dear. She, too, must be exhausted. I hoped my panic and fears had not overburdened her. A couple of students said they also were feeling at the end of their strength. Perhaps we were all near wits' end. Following this brief communal commiseration, the Abbess went on with her talk, though I don't remember what she said.

After lunch, to clear my mind, I walked down the monastery path to listen to the soothing burbling of Tassajara Creek. Slowly I realized that a transformative breakthrough wasn't going to happen for me this Rohatsu. As much as I longed for deeper understanding, as many years as I had committed absolutely to trying my hardest, I knew I didn't have anything more to give. Odious as it felt to capitulate, I had to admit that practice period was over for me. I was broken. I didn't even know if I could continue to practice Zen. Maybe I was not hardcore enough. Maybe I was "Zen-lite." The job now was to get through to the end. Forget enlightenment. Just lighten up.

That night I woke up at 2:30 a.m. to pee but decided to stay in bed because there was only one hour until I would get up for zazen. Big mistake. Thoughts of being trapped in Tassajara's mountainous ravine invaded my mind. Panic rose in my chest and throat. I turned on the light so I could get my bearings. I tried to sleep, but I was too agitated. I waited. Slowly the panic subsided. I decided I must stop following the schedule or else leave Tassajara. I wrote a note to the Abbess to put on her cushion, asking to see her, as she had invited me to do. Shakily, I started another day in the zendo.

In the short interval at the end of the first period of zazen, the Abbess came to my seat and guided me to her meeting room. When we sat down facing each other there, she gazed at me kindly. She gently asked a series of questions to assess my condition—"Where in your body do you feel the panic?"

"In the throat and chest and stomach."

"What are the sensations that you have?"

"Pressure, blockage, feelings of not being able to get enough air."

"How long do they last?"

"I don't know exactly. Maybe two or three minutes."

"What helps them to go away?"

"Breathing, taking slow, deep breaths. Concentrating on relaxing my stomach."

"Have you had panic attacks before? Did you suffer any trauma in your childhood that might be coming up now?"

"No, I haven't had anything that I could call an actual panic attack, though some weeks ago there were a couple of times when I felt claustrophobic. I feel so confined here. I feel I must get out of Tassajara as soon as possible. In zazen I have been hating Zen. I feel trapped. I want to see the ocean. I feel I should give up Zen, I should turn in my okesa. I'm afraid I might stand up and scream and run out of the zendo. I don't know how I can get through Rohatsu."

The Abbess studied me quietly for a few moments and then said, "I think you need to get out of the zendo for part of each day. Do you think doing some other activities throughout the day might help ground you?—like sewing or cooking or drawing or walking?"

We discussed each of these. We agreed on a plan to vary my activities so I could steady myself, and also have more interaction with other people. She said I could come and go as needed in the zendo. Then she advised, "Stay with the panicky feeling when it arises. Don't touch it, but don't turn away from it. Don't analyze it or label it; just be with it."

"I have been feeling anxious about the world going on without me. That being here is like being dead." I admitted with an embarrassed smile. "I know, of course, the world *will* and *does* go on without me."

"Yes, this might be at the bottom of your panic—fear of death," she replied gently.

That made sense. I did fear I might collapse. My entire body longed to give up, to lie down and curl into oblivion. Because I believed I must go on, I kept trying. The panic attacks were the body's intervention in the mind's determination. The body insisted that I stop or I might not survive. I thought of the beautiful lines from the *Eihei Koso Hotsuganmon* sutra:

Those who in past lives were not enlightened will now be enlightened.
In this life, save the body which is the fruit of many lives.
Before buddhas were enlightened, they were the same as we.
Enlightened people of today are exactly as those of old.

The tenderness of the phrase, *save the body*, brought tears to my eyes now. With those words, I accepted that in order to keep going, I must stop struggling. In these final weeks my entire focus had become the body, resting it as much as the schedule allowed, moving it to get as much exercise as fatigue would allow, strengthening and stretching it in daily yoga so I could Just Keep Going to the End of Practice Period. *Save the Body* now meant giving the body permission to stop, to rest. It meant letting go of longing for enlightenment. Accepting the body and its limitations. Accepting and honoring them.

The Zen tradition of sitting zazen is to be fully in the present moment (which continuously changes), not to seek something beyond it. Acceptance of continuous change frees us from suffering. Monastic training, however, encourages monks to practice with zeal, continually trying our hardest to break through the bondage of our preferences. This admonition can be mistaken for the ambition for enlightenment. I had spent many years caught in this paradox of trying to live in the present while vigorously stretching for the ultimate. Although in zazen I have had numerous moments of insight and contentment, in old age my response to the encouragement to try harder has been to feel a failure. Now nearing the end of practice period, I had to face that I was unable either to live in the moment or to keep pushing. I felt a miserable failure—not the outcome I wanted from all the effort and focus practice period had demanded. How to go forward?

After breakfast, the Abbess came to my room. "Take a walk outside and look at things that are beautiful," she said. "Perhaps draw if you want (she knew I liked to paint). I will talk with the Tenzo and others to see if you can work in the kitchen and also do some sewing." These were highly unusual modifications to make, especially for iconic Rohatsu. How fortunate I was to be at Tassajara when the Abbess was leading the practice. From the start, I admired her quiet but confident leadership as she firmly guided this historically masculine institution. Now her compassion revealed her deeply feminine nature as well. She was the perfect teacher to help me.

On returning to the zendo for afternoon zazen, I found a note stating that I was to have practice discussion with the Tanto the next day. I was alarmed. I hadn't requested a meeting, as was the protocol. Had I done something wrong again? Then I realized he might be meeting with each of the Tangaryo students as part of his leadership responsibilities. I must think of a question to ask him, as he might expect.

That night, despite my weariness, I couldn't get to sleep. Gradually I became aware of how bright and vibrant it was outside. Through the window I saw the stars twinkling in the night sky and the moon so bright it seemed to be shouting, "Wake up! Wake up!" It was near midnight, but I could hear monks walking around, coming and going to the zendo. On the night before the final day of Rohatsu, in emulation of the historical Buddha, who sat day and night until he reached enlightenment, students were invited to do zazen into the night—to wake up, as the Buddha had. What a powerful night it was. What a powerful place Tassajara was.

The next morning even without sufficient sleep, I didn't feel tired. During the morning meal chant, when we said, "May we realize the emptiness of the Three Wheels" (original teachings of the Buddha) I realized that my claustrophobia and panic were empty (of permanence), too. They were just limbic responses, perhaps from deep in my life/childhood, that I could just observe and then release. Perhaps they were the primitive energy of the dream leopard reflexively trying to protect me. No abiding reality to them. I felt my mind relax a bit.

Later the Abbess gave a lovely dharma talk on being kind to our bodies. She told us that leaving home, relinquishing our usual life to go live as monks, meant leaving our fixed views of things. We were learning to let everything be just as it was, moment to moment—including ourselves, our bodies. She recommended that we treat our bodies, as well as everything and everyone else, with kindness. With her help, I was finally focused on being kind to my exhausted body and mind.

After the dharma talk, the Tanto's assistant told me to go meet with him. I went to his practice discussion room. Knocking and entering, I bowed to the Buddha statue, then to the Tanto, and then sat down on the zafu facing him. After arranging my robes, I placed my hands in the mudra and looked up at him. He gazed directly at me for a long while.

Thinking that though he had requested our meeting, he might be waiting for me to speak, I said, "Thank you for facilitating my stay here. Without the accommodations you have provided for me to rest and work, I could not have done this practice period."

The Tanto nodded in agreement. We shared a rueful smile.

"I'm worn down to a nub now," I said.

"That's the point," he chuckled, "though not really."

Silence ensued.

Wondering how to proceed, I tried diplomacy: "This has been a big experience."

Finally he said, "I must give you some feedback on how properly to wear your priest's robes. I did not tell Nomon (Tim) that I would train you, but I feel you should know that you have not been properly attired while here."

I was taken aback, but there was no room in this tiny space to sit further from him. I remained upright and prepared to listen carefully to whatever he would say.

"You have not been wearing your juban correctly," he said. "Its white collar should always be visible just above the gray collar of the kimono, and yours has not been. Moreover, it is not proper to wear a turtleneck shirt beneath robes, and definitely one should not wear a cloak or cape over one's robes. In fact, nothing should be worn over the okesa—no shawl for warmth, no raincoat."

"I had not realized the rule about not covering the okesa, but I did know I shouldn't wear a turtleneck," I admitted, my voice squeaking a bit. "I did so in order to keep warm in the mornings. As for the juban, I have struggled to make it show just above the kimono collar. I know I have failed in this. I apologize. Thank you for the feedback."

I was confused. Why had he waited until the end of practice period to give me this feedback? Perhaps sensing my confusion, the Tanto described some clever ways to keep warm while still wearing one's robes correctly and elegantly. They were good ideas I hadn't heard before. With further thank you's, I bowed out of our meeting and returned to the dorm, a bit bruised but also grateful to have been instructed. And to have taken his admonitions in stride. This was the monastic pedagogy, and mine was the monk's life.

Later that day I mused on the Tanto's message. My sense was that he—and maybe others in responsible roles—might not have been happy that I was included in practice period. They might have worried, understandably enough, that I would have health problems or an accident that would require an emergency response. This would be difficult from Tassajara's remote location. The road out was long and rough. The terrain was so steep and rugged, I'd been told, that a medical helicopter could not land there. Or perhaps the accommodation I'd needed was just a perturbation in the normal operations of the monastery and thereby an annoyance. I wondered why I had been permitted to come. Several times the Abbess had expressed her appreciation for my presence. The Abiding Teacher also seemed to appreciate what my unusual age added to the mix. Although everyone eventually got used to and pretty much accepted me, I wondered if I had had much positive impact. I concluded morosely that I might not be alone in feeling it inappropriate for me to be at Tassajara.

With the Abbess's support I did make it to the end of Rohatsu. Early the last morning we celebrated the Buddha's Enlightenment with a rousing ceremony. While two monks beat rhythmically on both sides of a taiko drum in the zendo, we marched around in a wavering line to its thunderous accompaniment. We chanted in Japanese, "Han Nya Ha Ra Mit Ta" (*Prajna Paramita*, meaning the Perfection of Wisdom). We flung colorful flower petals into the air and onto the cushions and floor. Some young monks were jubilant, shouting, dancing, and whirling as we marched around and around the zendo. It was fun, a welcome release of pent-up energy from our intense Rohatsu effort.

Following oryoki breakfast in the zendo, we moved on to the Personal Day schedule with the usual activities of laundry, Bath, and room cleaning, to which we added packing for departure four days hence. We could break the silence and talk with each other. The Abbess advised us to allow people to engage when and if they wanted and to let alone anyone who wanted to be quiet. I was blitzed from the stress of sesshin week and spoke to no one the entire morning. As the day passed, however, I relaxed and eventually joined in conversation with others. I also picked up my mail. I had seven letters to savor, two of which I answered using the last two pieces of paper in the stationery pad I had brought to Tassajara. How well I had planned the logistics of the experience. How little I had controlled its substance.

Resting in the dorm that afternoon, I thought about the physical place of Tassajara. The intense, rough energy of the rugged mountainside, contrasted with the lush vegetation of the narrow valley, made the setting spectacular. The mountainsides loomed over the monastery, pressing right up to the back walls of some of its buildings. Numerous boulders lying beside the walking path attested to thundering rock falls in the past. And threatened that future boulders might also crash down. Many of the younger monks loved the intensity of the setting, but it unsettled me. In visits to Tassajara many years earlier, I had not felt endangered. But now in old age, less agile and accordingly more cautious, I was uncomfortable. The physical place was too powerful for me.

The final full day of practice period, now mid-December, arrived. In the late morning, the community met in the Conference Center for almost two hours. We sat on uncomfortable metal folding chairs in a big circle around the perimeter of the room. The Abbess invited everyone to say anything we wanted in farewell to the practice period. I was glad to get this late, small taste of the many monks I had not gotten to know. When my turn came, I said, "Thank you, everyone, for your support and the accommodations you have made for me. I know some of you had to substitute for me on serving crews. I am sorry to have caused you extra work. Thank you, everyone, for getting me through to this day before the last day," I laughed self-consciously. A few monks kindly chuckled in sympathy.

In the circle as I listened, I wondered if I would miss Tassajara. I thought probably not. Over practice period I had been dimly aware that various individuals were suffering—a young woman who sobbed in anguish in her room one afternoon but refused offers of help; a young man and his wife, both of whom were frequently sick in bed; the very depressed man I had asked about; a woman priest who was often out of the zendo, presumably ill. As time passed, my own suffering increasingly demanded my attention. By the final weeks I was no longer capable of offering others compassion. All I could do was push the body toward the end and go home.

We weren't given a list of practice period participants, as often happens at the end of conferences or gatherings of people from different places. I didn't think to request one, an omission I later regretted. It would have helped me remember the other monks more easily. Perhaps, though, losing connection with others was another lesson in *no self.* As I live my regular life immersed in friendships and family connections, it is not so obvious, as it was at Tassajara, that like all things, relationships are ephemeral, only moment to moment.

On December 20 we left Tassajara at last. Three vans full of Tangaryo students and some residents headed out at 8:40 a.m. I sat between two dorm mates, comforted to be with friends. I was also relieved to find our driver was a Tangaryo student, a gentle young man who was an EMT. He could negotiate the tortuous Tassajara road, as well as the hectic freeway traffic north to San Francisco. My anxiety level reduced, I would doze on and off during our four-hour trip.

At the top of Tassajara Road, we stopped at Jamesburg, where we could stretch our legs. We said the goodbyes we hadn't said before departing the monastery. Two of the practice leaders who were also in the vans gave me warm hugs. I realized that though they hadn't expressed it, they must have felt some empathy for me and everyone else who struggled these past three months. This comforted me as now I aimed disconsolately toward home. I would stay overnight at City Center—an appreciated part of the Tassajara "package deal"—before flying out on Saturday morning back home to Bellingham.

Chapter Fifteen

Study the Self

Four days before Christmas, 10:00 p.m. I dragged luggage and weary body from the taxi into my cold, dark house, turned the furnace back on, made toast and tea, took a hot bath, and slept for twelve hours. Next morning, naked after a shower, I glanced in the bathroom mirror to behold a gaunt face, thin arms, shrunken breasts, protruding ribs. Shocked, I weighed myself. I had lost twenty-two pounds. I had felt thinner toward the end of practice period, but I had no idea I'd lost so much weight. The monastic schedule left no time for even quick mirror checks, plus my voluminous robes masked any bodily changes I might have noticed. I had eaten well at Tassajara and never felt hungry. Sleep deprivation must have done it. Anger welled up in me: the ordination requirement to practice at Tassajara might have damaged my health.

For the first two or three weeks back home, sleep was the priority. I went to bed at 8 p.m. and took afternoon naps. I restarted civilian life—sorted mail, washed clothes, paid bills. On Christmas Day, I called Alec and Dan in Florida, comforted to speak with family again.

I felt breathless and dizzy much of the time, emotionally whiplashed. Frequently I found myself in tears—of exhaustion, relief. I returned to yoga and swimming gradually, though because of a shoulder tendonitis I had developed toward the end of practice period, for several weeks I had to do deep-water running instead of swimming laps. This was a repetitive motion injury from putting on and taking off my okesa multiple times every day for ninety days. The required backward shoulder rotations eventually became too much for my aging body. I bet younger priests did not develop this malady.

Through January I gradually returned to physical balance, but mental instability dragged on. I railed against the institutional requirement to go to

Tassajara in order to be ordained. I berated myself for having submitted to it. I built my case by looking up the effects of sleep deprivation on the elderly and found among them what I had experienced the third month: exhaustion, confusion, irritability, anxiety, depression. Lack of sleep had unhinged me.

I was relieved to be home, but my mind wasn't functioning normally. I couldn't focus on anything for long. Was this because I'd spent three months assiduously focused on the present moment, or had I lost it? Sometimes as I set out in the car I couldn't remember where I was going. I complained bitterly to friends about Tassajara, baffling those who knew little about Zen and could not imagine monastic life would be anything but serene. My brain's executive control center seemed to be malfunctioning. What would it take to recover? I had come close to a mental breakdown, and I was damn mad about it.

By late January I began to feel more like my old self. I'd regained some weight and no longer looked like I'd come out of the Dust Bowl. The shoulder tendonitis had improved. Then one Saturday night when leaving a dinner party, I missed an unlighted, final, walkway step and pitched forward onto the grassy public right-of-way, falling hard on my tendonitis shoulder. I was able to push myself up, crawl to the car, and drive home, but it was clear the shoulder was seriously injured. Later the diagnosis was a badly torn rotator cuff.

All through February and well into spring, I focused on repairing my shoulder. At first I could not raise that arm above my head, so I couldn't swim laps. I continued the deep water running. I had weekly treatments of physical therapy, deep tissue massage, and chiropractic. I sat in the sauna and steam rooms at the Y twice a week. At Tassajara, as I had grown more fatigued, my focus had been increasingly on taking care of the body. Now, ironically, saving the body continued to be my practice. I paid close attention to how I lifted and carried objects, got in and out of the car, and turned the steering wheel. These weeks of nursing my shoulder initiated me into actual old age, as ever since, I have had to spend more of my daily life attending to self-care.

As the months of recuperation passed, I wondered why at Tassajara I had not put my health before my presumed responsibilities as a priest. Why had I felt compelled to follow the rigorous monastery regimen even when I believed it was harmful? I'd chafed at the demanding schedule, but I couldn't bring myself to disobey it. Partly, this was out of long habit. When young and strong, I had enthusiastically obeyed the Zen admonition to try my hardest. I had thrilled to the challenge of exerting body and mind in search of insight and happiness.

My Western, Christian upbringing did not include warrior energy as an ideal, but similar inner reserves must have served me in the challenges I'd faced in adolescence and marriage. Now in old age and no longer capable of

Zen warrior exertion, I had to face the fact that I couldn't fulfill the expectations of the very institution I had been devoted to for over forty years. As a priest, not being able to follow the schedule completely meant not being acceptable, my deepest fear. I railed against this unwanted change. Why hadn't I simply refused to go to Tassajara? I knew it would be too difficult. Why had I given in without trying harder to negotiate? I hadn't seen I had a choice. How pathetic was that? This struggle would finally resolve itself: I could not intentionally disobey the schedule, but I could fail, trying my best to follow it.

Now back home where I could take care of my body, finally things began to fall into a more realistic perspective. My experience at Tassajara had revealed that for my entire life I'd had a distorted view of myself in relation to other people. At last I knew I was *not* an unacceptable being, as I had concluded in adolescence. I did not have to prove my worth by always doing what was expected. I wished I had realized much earlier how driven I was since adolescence by fear of rejection. But I was deeply grateful to have uncovered this pernicious, neurotic character knot of fear and submission. And grateful to Zen and Tassajara for revealing it to me.

I had expected to be "done" with Tassajara once I left it, but I continued to ponder the powerful experiences I'd had there. The Director had told us Tangaryo monks we might not realize all we had learned until afterward. To understand what happened more deeply, I began writing down what I recollected, describing the activities and analyzing their effects on me. Soon I realized I was following the seminal teaching of Dogen Zenji, the 13th century founder of the Soto school of Zen in Japan:

> To study the Way is to study the Self.
> To study the Self is to forget the Self.
> To forget the Self is to become intimate with all things.

I was excited to find the writing came easily, sometimes in floods of words. It helped me understand what I had experienced. It was healing. I returned to pondering the dream leopard that had startled me awake midway through practice period. That dream had to be related to my rage at Sherry, but it had occurred more than a week *before* that incident, so it wasn't in reaction to it. Initially I had thought it represented fear, but now it seemed more like defensive anger. Perhaps anger about Sherry's rejection had been building in me without my awareness, and the dream was its forecast.

I wondered what in me the leopard represented. Online research said that leopards are powerfully aggressive when threatened but live peacefully and hunt by themselves in the jungle or forest. They are solitaries, with the strengths and strategies to take care of themselves. I, too, preferred solitude. I may have been drawn to Zen practice because it demanded a strong, personal commitment, and also because in the silence of zazen I could be safe while with others. The adage is that the leopard can't change its spots. In adolescence I couldn't change my back condition and brace. But rather than protecting me as the leopard's spots camouflaged her, my "spots" caused me to stand out and be attacked. This puzzling twist in the comparison made the dream leopard hard to interpret.

My leopard energy could be tricky. It could give me the appearance, quite falsely, of self-confidence. Friends and family could never square my apparent enterprising nature with my frequent anxiety about failing—to pass a Master's degree orals exam, to manage a solo trip to Europe, to speak effectively at a professional meeting. If I appeared so confident (possibly still "rising above it"), why was I so anxious? I never understood this contradiction myself until after Tassajara. When reflecting on the leopard's meaning, I saw how its energy had both masked a lack of self-confidence and fueled an equally strong determination to succeed.

My leopard energy seemed to both enable and disable me. In adolescence its power allowed me to fight off and survive peer rejection. But its solitary nature encouraged me to withdraw from community rather than demand my rights, a choice that trapped me in dysfunctional behavior and relationships.

For my entire life, up until Tassajara, I was confused by the contradictory nature of the impulses to both succeed and recede. Because these opposing impulses struggled below my conscious awareness, I did not understand them or the anxiety I perpetually felt. This struggle prevented using the full resources of my mind and heart to make important life decisions concerning marriage, motherhood, and most broadly, trusting other people. The unconscious leopard energy protected me from feeling shame and anger, but it also prevented my being whole.

This dueling must have been loosening over the many years of Zen practice. Finally at Tassajara the rigid scaffolding on which I had constructed and conducted relationships broke through to consciousness and tumbled down around me. Once I returned home and began to write about Tassajara, it was this wreckage that I would sift through, examine, and use to understand my life.

I was shocked to realize how much my unconscious mind had limited me in receiving love and loving others. But I was also relieved to understand why loving relationships had been elusive. To discover this deeply buried, pernicious complex and its jujitsu around love was transformational. At last I could begin to forgive myself for making poor choices.

I knew being bullied in adolescence had badly frightened and humiliated me. Now I was beginning to see it had also deeply angered me without my realizing it. Back in 1948 well brought up girls were taught to be courteous and submissive. Anger might have been so unacceptable then that I could not consciously feel it, let alone express it. I resorted to the more culturally acceptable feminine behaviors of compliance and self-denial. It was only at Tassajara, a lifetime later, when my early conditioning to seek acceptance surfaced, that the long-buried anger also appeared, symbolized by the leopard.

My unexpected rage at Sherry did feel familiar. I had experienced similar explosions a few times before, each associated with feeling humiliated. In high school civics class I proposed an action for our class to take. I mistakenly thought others supported the idea, so I confidently declared, "We all agree that. . . ." Interrupting me, the whole class cried out, "No, we don't!" I sat down immediately, overcome and furious at myself for having misread the situation. Another unexpected explosion of rage occurred when I was around twenty-five. My first husband and I were at a summer beach party in his hometown. People were drinking and the party was getting rough. Feeling uneasy, I asked to go home, but he bluntly dismissed me, complaining that I was such a drag to be with. Again, humiliation at being "in the wrong" washed over me, followed immediately by hot anger, which, fearing further rejection, I swallowed. A few days later, I developed a painful lump in my esophagus. Its cause was diagnosed as stress, and I was prescribed tranquilizers.

Apparently from adolescent years onward, I couldn't tolerate feeling either anger or humiliation (or its deeper sibling, shame), so I suppressed both emotions. Whenever I was exposed as "wrong," however, I re-experienced the physical sensations and emotions I had felt when bullied—perhaps as post-traumatic stress symptoms. Rage quickly followed as the antidote, which just as quickly I also suppressed. I never acknowledged or integrated these powerful emotions until at Tassajara when, for three months, I sat with Sherry's silent rejection.

I wanted to untie the pernicious psychic knot of shame and anger lodged in my unconscious since youth. I read some Jungian psychology and found a useful definition of psychological complexes in *The Wild Edge of Sorrow* by Francis Weller, who wrote—

> Complexes are fragmentary bundles of concentrated emotional energy formed when we were confronted with an experience too intense for us to successfully digest. In these moments, the psyche splinters off the difficult material and creates an autonomous, semi-contained bundle to hold the highly charged material. . . . Our psyches dissociate, splitting off the offending material from consciousness for the time being.

But if we are to become psychologically whole, Weller warns, eventually we must face and integrate the suppressed material. "Until we do," he concludes, quoting Jung, 'the complex will interfere with the intentions of our will and disturb the conscious performance.'" (Weller 2015, 5–6).

This definition of complexes and how they interfere with our conscious intentions and behavior, distorting and confusing our motives, was the insight I had been seeking. At Tassajara I was awakened to my suppressed rage through both the leopard dream and my alarming reaction to Sherry's dismissal. To make sense of the dream leopard's message, I had to examine the "charged material" of my unconscious and accept that it had shaped my life. When I embarked on this memoir, I thought I would just recount the challenges and rewards of my Zen experiences. But Tassajara and the dream leopard brought together two important realizations: my lifelong, desperate need for acceptance, and the shame and anger I had harbored since adolescence because I believed I was unacceptable. These twinned insights have relieved me of confusion and self-recrimination and made it possible to have compassion for myself—the Bodhisattva vow I had taken as a priest but seldom applied to myself.

The Bodhisattva is an archetype of Mahayana Buddhism, the tradition underlying Soto Zen. A Bodhisattva is enlightened and therefore could leave this suffering world forever, but out of compassion for others, she remains in the world to save all suffering beings first. The Bodhisattva ideal is incorporated into Zen practice as the expression of the wisdom and compassion cultivated in zazen. At Red Cedar Zen Center and many other Soto Zen centers, the Bodhisattva vows are chanted following dharma talks. They express our realization that we are all interrelated. In helping others, we help ourselves. The extravagant goals of these vows reveal the inner Buddha nature to which Bodhisattvas are encouraged to aspire:

Beings are numberless, I vow to save them.
Delusions are inexhaustible, I vow to end them.
Dharma gates are boundless, I vow to enter them.
Buddha's way is unsurpassable, I vow to become it.

In Buddhism, the concept of No Self is fundamental. The mistaken belief that we have a self, the teachings say, is the cause of our suffering. The way our minds work makes us believe there is a distinct, unchanging being (self) that experiences events, actions, and other beings. The truth is that like all phenomena, we are always changing, dependent on with what and whom we're interacting. There is no such thing as an ongoing, unchanging being. Thus Buddhism says there is No Self. This fundamental impermanence is an especially difficult concept for people in our Western, materialist, individualist, and competitive culture to understand. Who is it that is competing, we argue, if not a separate, distinct being called "I"?

Early in my Zen practice, I was drawn to the idea of No Self, but for many years I couldn't digest it, couldn't feel it in my body. I intuited that No Self promised liberation from the inner demons I struggled with but could not name. Eventually I came to understand cognitively that the Self has no abiding, continuous existence. Emotionally, however, this knowledge just wouldn't stick until my experiences at Tassajara revealed my unconscious misunderstanding.

Back home from Tassajara and examining the leopard dream, I realized that the leopard's role might not have been to protect me from the unkindness of others. It might have been to *deflect* me from feeling the fear, anger, and shame I deeply but unconsciously felt in response. Unable to access these painful feelings, I could not integrate them into my conscious mind or persona. I did sense that something was underneath my conscious awareness, but I thought it must be my hidden Self (the one Buddhism teaches does not exist).

I saw now that what I had *inferred* as a Self was not a self at all. It was a neurotic complex of suppressed, unassimilated assumptions about my relation to others. Leopard energy sometimes protected this complex from outside threat; other times it blinded me to its neurotic nature. These insights solved the Buddhist puzzle of No Self for me. More amazing, they solved the enigma of personal suffering. I had long understood the Emptiness of All Things (meaning nothing has abiding qualities or nature, so let's not cling and thereby suffer). Now I could feel the emptiness of (my) Being. I could experience everything, including "myself," as what it is in the moment without expectations of what it will become. As the Tassajara leaders taught us, I could rely on Not Knowing and Just Being. As Dogen taught, at last I could appreciate that *to forget the Self is to become intimate with all things.*

Chapter Sixteen

Fifty Years in Zen

Five years have passed since my powerful experience at Tassajara. Red Cedar Zen Center in Bellingham is thriving—serene and welcoming. Many new people have come through our doors on Wednesday evenings to attend orientations, try out two periods of zazen followed by chanting, bowing, and a dharma talk. Some newcomers are college-aged, but more are middle-aged and older, seeking peace and solace in culturally turbulent times. We guide them to watch their mind and let go of thinking. We suggest they count their breaths as a way to center themselves. We show them how to sit cross-legged on zafus on the floor in the compact form that is the traditional posture for zazen. It collects and grounds the body and focuses the mind. It fosters humility and right relationship with all beings, a tender interconnectedness with others, the heart of sangha life.

These years have been full of changes in both my Zen practice and daily life. Old age has arrived. It has influenced my practice and aroused my curiosity about how to continue to grow spiritually. It is commonly understood that growing old entails slowing down and doing less—two conditions most of us fight as long as possible. Elizabeth Kubler-Ross's famous model of the five stages of grief—denial, anger, bargaining, depression, and acceptance—captures my experience of aging. When I find I can no longer do something important to me, typically I don't realize at first that I must adapt. I deny and resist. When I do realize I must change, I feel upset (angry). Often I blame someone or something for my discomfort or I bargain to not have to change. Finally I feel discouraged, even depressed, before I give up and accept that I must change. My first month at Tassajara was full of these feelings.

As I cycle through these stages of letting go, I am cognizant that the solution is to accept the new reality as soon as possible. To come to peace with a significant change, however, I have found I must experience grief for the loss or restriction before I can let go and embrace a new, often less desirable, condition or activity.

I have had to make changes in my daily activities because of pain and increasing mobility restrictions: Hip pain caused me to change my transportation habits. I could no longer walk the half-mile to the bus stop, so as foolish as it seemed, I began driving to the stop, parking, and then taking the bus. A year later, I could no longer walk from the bus depot to downtown destinations. Reluctantly I began driving the car, rationing trips to one per day and grateful to be reducing my carbon footprint on the occasional day I didn't leave home. Next, hip pain and declining balance led me to need a cane, a sure sign of old age I was reluctant to demonstrate, but now I am grateful for the mobility it provides. I need more sleep now than I used to. This means I have less time to do things I want to do. So I am cutting back on some commitments. That way I can still attend to priest activities I regard as highest priority, such as meeting with Zen friends in mentoring and study sessions.

My close attention to declining mobility is driven partly by the fact that my two older sisters and mother each became wheelchair-bound in their eighties due to lumbar nerve impingements like mine. I am anxious to avoid their fate for as long as possible. That said, I am surprised to discover that old age is a time of almost continuous change, requiring frequent adjustments to our expectations and activities. Such changes require both diligence and skill to manage well. Old age is a time when one needs an *agile* mind, contrary to the stereotype that the old are closed-minded. Happily, Zen training in observing the mind comes to our rescue. Old age is the perfect opportunity to live in the present moment where there are plenty of challenges to meet and resolve.

Pain and mobility problems have also required significant changes in my Zen practice. Doing zazen in a chair has been a big adjustment. I resisted and groused about this change for three or four years. I tried kneeling, lying down, even standing up. Whatever position I selected, I had to change it frequently in order to avoid exacerbating my pinched nerve and arthritis conditions. Changing positions disturbed nearby students, of course, so that was not the answer. More subtle but equally difficult to accept, sitting in a chair required an unexpected adjustment. I follow the Zen tradition of keeping my eyes softly open during zazen. From a chair the visual field is much larger than from a zafu. Forms and movements more easily distract and trigger unwanted speculations about their causes and significance. I've had to learn to guard the mind much more energetically than from a zafu where I could gaze at the blank floor or wall.

By far the most painful change in my practice has been giving up sesshins. The long days of zazen became too tiring and actually harmful to my fragile low back. Being mobile is now essential for me to stay strong and keep pain at bay. In addition to exercising daily, all day long I need to be able to stretch, twist, bend, and sit in various kinds of chairs, as well as walk, and lie down. Sitting still for hours in zazen is *exactly* counter to what my body needs. It is a brutal irony that after all these years of practice, culminating in ordination, I have had to choose between traditional Zen practice and physical health. Practice now must be in service of my body, rather than the other way around. Fortunately, I have learned that zazen mind resides not just on the zafu. It can go anywhere.

Cutting out sesshins has been necessary, but it has come at a big price. I no longer have access to the emotional and psychic depths that continuous days of zazen offer. Worse, I have lost the deep connection with sangha friends that comes from making the great, shared effort sesshins require. Emotionally, I have traveled to the periphery of sangha life as I knew and loved it for nearly fifty years. This has been a difficult transition, with some bitter moments, going from practice leadership to sangha bit player. As I came to realize I must make this major change, I went through the grief cycle: blaming the institution for insisting on long sesshin days; trying to participate in only part of sesshins; complaining to close sangha friends about missing sesshins. I finally accepted and completed this adjustment, but I still experience moments of poignant loss. Aging has become my charge now—saving the body, the priority, doing it gracefully, my quest.

During these years of sorrowfully withdrawing from the heart of Zen practice, I faced another conundrum. As a priest, I wanted and felt I was expected to contribute in a significant way to the sangha. I struggled with how to do this within my physical capacities. Finally, I realized I could contribute to the organizational side of our community. I volunteered as Red Cedar's Board President. Over two and a half years I worked with the board to develop needed policies for the building lease and rental, a policy and procedure for evaluating the sangha's guiding teacher, and finalized a years' long effort to create a sangha communications policy.

In a response to the 2016 presidential election, I was drawn to focus my organization and administrative skills on national and state politics. For two years, daily I researched, called, and wrote congressional representatives to convey my views and requests about national issues such as climate change, health care, gun violence, and ethics in government. In the occasional dharma talks I gave during this time, I encouraged sangha members to use Buddhist principles of right speech and right action for political action. This was Bodhisattva work, and I could do it from home where I could sit, stand, or walk as needed. I also led community workshops created by the national volunteer organization, Better Angels, on how to communicate with people on the other side of the political spectrum. These activities allowed me to be productive and helped dispel the disappointment of being a priest without the expected portfolio.

As a priest I can serve as the Doshi, leading Zen services. This role involves walking ceremonially back and forth between the bowing mat and the altar several times during chanting; and standing and bowing during the service numerous times. If I am unsteady walking that evening (which can occur unexpectedly), my role requires a group effort. I ask the Ino or Jisha to move a chair up behind the bowing mat so I can sit during parts of the service. Often I also must do standing bows rather than the expected full prostrations. This involves alerting the Doan ringing the bells so her timing is not thrown off by my abbreviated bow. At first, I was embarrassed to reveal my disability and old age so obviously, but the sangha has been kind in helping when needed. In a sweet way, we're all being Doshi together, and they get to see that physical limitations don't prohibit practice.

As a priest I also meet with students individually in practice discussions some Wednesday evenings and as a mentor, monthly, with two or three students each year. Occasionally I teach a class or give a dharma talk. I can perform all priestly duties except for ordinations, which are conducted only by fully authorized priests. I am oldest in years among the Red Cedar priests and even longest in Zen practice, but I am lowest in rank due to their originally being ordained before I was. This is the tradition in Zen, a sometimes irksome feature. But mostly it suits me to occupy a humble station. I like to be reminded to drop the demanding ego self. Humility does not prevent offering what I want to offer—encouraging Zen practice and the Bodhisattva Way.

During the transition away from sesshins, I kept an eye open for other needs I might fill as a priest. I discovered some sangha members were feeling less able to practice in the traditional way. With Tim's encouragement, I developed and taught two one-day "Gentle Zen" retreats on practicing with limitations, plus a five-evening course on "Death and Dying" that I co-led with three other senior students. A year or so later, I heard from a few more members that they were struggling with some of our zendo forms. I convened two focus groups to discuss their concerns. Together we suggested small changes our sangha could institute to make it easier for people with limitations to practice at the zendo. One that was easy to implement was inviting students with back or leg pain to lie down during dharma talks. Another was providing a little more time for getting up after zazen for those with stiff backs and limbs.

More recently I led a study group on Shantideva's *Way of the Bodhisattva*, using Pema Chodron's guide, *Becoming Bodhisattvas* (2018). In twelve monthly meetings, we challenged ourselves to adapt Shantideva's hearty admonitions to not cause harm through speech or action by remaining "like a log of wood." Being steady and patient allows us to overcome bad habits and be of benefit to others. We found Shantideva's youthful zeal for disciplining the mind good medicine for old age and its tendency to give up trying to live as fully as we can.

Shantideva's advice for intervening in harmful thinking before we act on it is particularly pertinent for elders. Typically we are less active in the world and have more time to study the mind than when we were younger and busier. We also face new, unwanted changes, and we have more opportunities to intervene earlier in our negative reactions. We don't have to cycle through all the stages of grief. First (Shantideva advises), through mindfulness we can try to catch the preverbal stage of emotional arousal, just the feeling, and breathe it out. Missing that, when a negative emotion begins to gain strength, we can intervene by deliberately letting it go. If we find we are beginning silently to verbalize a negative thought, we can stop the words in our mind. Finally, if we realize we are about to speak or act in a harmful way, we can strongly intervene and stop ourselves. The teaching is to observe the mind in each of these conditions, training it to acknowledge and intervene in negativity before acting on it. This way we don't harm others or ourselves. Perhaps the practice for the elderly is Intensive Mindfulness—good at any age but especially useful for the unwanted changes elders can experience.

The changes I have had to make these past five years have demonstrated that elders can still have agency, even if in a shrinking arena. Helping others continue to practice and be vitally alive has become my mission as an octogenarian priest. In fact, the original American Zen students of the 1960s and 70s are now in our seventies and eighties. Isn't it time that we examine our rigorous practice forms to insure that they don't exclude elders? The question is not easily resolved: traditional Zen practice rightly enough emphasizes discipline and effort and zeal. But as devoted practitioners age and develop physical limitations, are we to be prohibited from sangha practice? Or are there roles we can take and practices we can do—and perhaps be encouraged to lead—as ways to continue our deep practice and commitment? Can we even find ways for our elders' wisdom to be useful to everyone? I hope American Zen centers are addressing these needs today.

As an elder Zen priest, I have changed not only my Zen practice, I've changed my mind. More accurately, my mind has changed *me*. The challenging experience at Tassajara and the process of writing this memoir have given me insights I never had before, despite many years of Zen practice and, intermittently, psychotherapy. Initially, I simply wanted to tell the story of how I came to Zen and what I have gained and treasured in its practice. To explain what happened to me at Tassajara, however, I needed to understand and integrate three aspects of that experience: the reasons why practice period was so hard for me; how the dharma teachings by the Tassajara practice leaders helped focus the experience; and the meaning of the interpersonal struggles I experienced there. Each of these aspects gave me new information about myself, and the Leopard dream tied things all together. As an arche-type, the Leopard took the most work to unpack and understand, but it contributed the most to my self-understanding.

During practice period I was supported by the dharma talks about how to work with the mind and in relationships with the other monks. The few conflicts I had at Tassajara yielded invaluable insights into my early condi-tioning. I came to see that all my life I had retained a defensive framework in relating to other people. When I saw these behaviors for what they were— helping people in order to be accepted, obeying those in power because I feared rejection or disapproval—I could drop them. The meaning of the leopard dream was more complex and took me the several years of writing this book to understand.

Finally I did understand: In adolescence I wrongly concluded from being bullied that I was *unworthy*. But because this was an unconscious conclusion, I didn't realize that it drove important life decisions such as whom to marry. Which in turn shaped not only my life but the lives of my children, and in ways I may never know, the lives of their children. From adolescence on-ward, I had no idea how deeply unconscious I was. I recognized that I had made bad decisions. I felt guilty and ashamed about the negative conse-quences those decisions had on me and my family's lives. But I did not understand that I could abandon those distorting misunderstandings. I could move on.

As an elder I am relieved to understand that these critical life decisions were driven by a deeply mistaken understanding of myself. I see now that I was *not* unacceptable. I did not purposely marry two men who could not love me. These were grievous mistakes, but they were *not* intentional. I no longer need to shoulder the self-condemnation I had carried. I feel sorrow, but I get to forgive myself. I am amazed and grateful beyond expression for this insight. I would never have achieved it if I hadn't written this memoir. It gave me the remarkable truth that liberation from early, negative condition-ing is possible and necessary.

Like all life, we human beings are always in process, changing over time. I found Zen in my late thirties and followed it into my eighties, slowly exploring and deepening my understanding—receiving the Precepts, becom-ing Head Student, taking the Priest's vow to support and encourage all be-ings. All those years I was becoming a little more realized and visible as a person, stepping forward to offer what I could, slowly learning to trust that others could receive me with kindness.

In old age I continue this journey of changing and becoming. It's true, now I must devote more attention to sustaining the body. I have less energy and more physical impairment, so my activities are more limited. But I also have the unexpected reward of a long life: solving the puzzle of "self"—in my case, a false, neurotic hologram, a phantom always just beyond my conscious reach.

Toward the end of Rohatsu, walking slowly down the silty path by Tassajara Creek, I realized I had to give up trying so hard. I had to accept that I had gone as far as I could. It wasn't quite the end of practice period, but my embodied self couldn't go any further. This had to be enough.

The truth is we *do* have to go as far as we can, but we don't have to go *farther* than that. The trick is, in order to discover we can't go farther, we have to go *exactly* to the point we can't go beyond. Therein lies liberation. There is Just Being.

Glossary of Terms

Abbess, Abbot	Head of a Monastery or Zen Center.
Dharma	The Buddha's teachings; ultimate reality or truth; also the facts.
Dharma name	Zen Practice name given by Zen teacher to a student in Jukai ceremony of commitment to Zen practice.
Doan	Ceremonial role of one who rings the bells for a Zen service.
Doan-ryo	Monks who lead chants and play bells and drums in the zendo for Zen services, rituals, and ceremonies—see Doan, Tenken, Kokyo.
Dogen, Eihei	13th C. founder of Soto Zen Buddhism in Japan.
Dokusan	Private, voluntary, formal meeting between a Zen student and the teacher, usually requested by the student.
Doshi	The priest officiating in services and ceremonies in the zendo.
Eight-Fold Path	The Way to practicing Buddhist teachings–Right View, Right Intention, Right Speech, Right Action, Right Livelihood, Right Effort, Right Concentration, Right Mindfulness.
Fukuten	Assistant to Head Cook (Tenzo). The Fukuten orders food, helps plan meals, and makes assignments to cook's helpers.
Gassho	A gesture of greeting—standing in half bow, palms pressed together in front of chest.

Han	A thick wooden slab struck with a mallet in a rhythmic pattern to call the monks to the zendo for zazen.
Hossenshiki	A ceremonial exchange of practice understanding between the Shuso (head student) and sangha members, held at the end of practice period.
Hyoshigi	Two five-inch hardwood sticks struck together making a sharp clap, to announce ceremonial events.
Ino	Zen officer in charge of zendo ceremonies and protocol.
Jika	A senior priest's attendant; arranges for meetings with students, does errands and administrative tasks.
Jisha	The Abbot/Abbess's attendant: arranges for meetings with students, does errands, assists with communications, and cleans robes and rooms, and so forth.
Juban	A white waist-length undergarment for priest's robes; its shawl collar shows just above robe's neck.
Jukai	The ceremony of commitment to the Precepts (Buddhist ethical principles) for lay Zen students.
Jundo	A ritual circumambulation of the zendo or the monastery altars in a half-crouch, hands in gassho.
Kaisando	Founder's Hall in a monastery or Zen temple/center.
Karma	The universal law of cause and effect saying every action has a consequence, so it is vital that we consider our actions carefully.
Karma Body	*or* Habit Body—the Abbess's term for our conditioned behavior.
Kimono	The ankle-length robe worn under the priest's formal koromo robe.
Kinhin	Slow walking meditation, usually done between periods of zazen.
Kokyo	The chant leader for services and ceremonies in the zendo.
Koromo	A priest's formal, black robe; has very long, draped sleeves.
Lay Entrustment	Ceremony for a very senior Zen lay practitioner authorizing him/her to teach but not to perform Zen services or ceremonies as priests do.
Makyo	Distracting visual or auditory illusions that can occur during zazen.

Mokugyo	The carved, wooden drum struck to keep the rhythm for some Zen chants.
Monastery Director	Administrator of a monastery, responsible for the physical plant and financial matters.
Okesa	Traditional priest's robe worn over koromo; hand-sewn by the priest in preparation for ordination; constructed of seven long panels, each made of three shorter panels. Worn over the left shoulder and wrapped around the body, to protect the koromo robe. Called the Buddha robe.
Oryoki	Traditional three nested eating bowls and ritual for meals in the zendo.
Paramitas	The Perfections or guides for Buddhist practice (generosity, ethics, patience, energy, concentration, wisdom).
Practice Period	A time of intensive monastic practice, usually three months, led by a senior teacher, usually in a Zen monastery or temple.
Rakusu	The bib-like vestment signifying lay commitment to Zen practice, sewn by the student in preparation for the Jukai ceremony.
Rinzai Zen	One of two main Zen sects, emphasizing rigorous practice, koan study and sudden enlightenment.
Rohatsu	The most sacred and rigorous sesshin honoring Buddha's enlightenment; occurs in early December.
Samu	Manual labor in the monastery or temple.
Samue	Monastery or temple work clothes.
Sangha	The name for a Buddhist community of monks, priests, teachers, and lay people.
Sanzen	Student's meeting in private with the teacher for instruction.
Seiza	The kneeling position for zazen.
Sesshin	A residential meditation retreat of several days or weeks.
Shashu	The position of the hands clasped at the waist when standing or walking in the zendo.
Shiho	Ceremonial granting to a novice priest the full authority to teach and conduct Zen services and ceremonies. Also called Transmission.

Shikantaza	Sitting upright in zazen, free from all conscious thoughts; defined by Dogen Zenji as *just sitting in awareness.*
Shosan ceremony	Ceremony at the end of a sesshin in which each student publicly asks the teacher a question about practice and receives an answer for all to contemplate.
Shoten	Bell ringer role to start and end the monastic meditation day.
Shuso	Head Student for a formal practice period—gives talks, helps students, answers questions in Hossenshiki ceremony at the end of practice period.
Soto Zen	One of two main Zen sects, emphasizing "just sitting" and the tradition of the Bodhissatva vow to save all beings.
Sutra	Discourses of the Buddha, chanted as part of Zen services.
Tabi	White, split-toe ankle socks worn for ceremonies.
Tan	The raised platform in the zendo on which students sit for zazen.
Tanto	The priest in charge of monks' training and decorum for practice period.
Tenken	The time keeper, signals the start and end of zazen periods.
Tenzo	The Head Cook.
Tokudo	The priest ordination ceremony.
Umpan	The flat metal gong used to call monks to meetings and meals.
Zabutan	The square, flat mat used for zazen.
Zafu	The round cushion for zazen, placed on top of the zabuton.
Zagu	The priest's bowing cloth, laid down on the floor to protect the priest's sacred okesa when the priest bows to the floor.
Zazen	Seated meditation.
Zen	Meditative state, absorption.
Zendo	Meditation Hall.

Bibliography

Aiken, Robert. 1984. *The Mind of Clover*. Berkeley, CA: North Point Press.

Bodhi, Bhikkhu. 2003. *A Comprehensive Manual of Abhidhamma*. Sri Lanka: Buddhist Publication Society.

Burnett, Nomon Tim. August 18, 2013. Unpublished Dharma talk for priest ordination ceremony (Shukke Tokudo).

Busch, Colleen Morton. 2008. *Fire Monks*. New York: Penguin Books.

Chodron, Pema. 2018. *Becoming Bodhisattvas*. Boulder, CO: Shambhala.

"Eihei Koso Hotsuganmon" at www.sfzc/offerings. Select Sutras; select Services, Sutras, Texts & Songs; select Daily Sutras, Verses and Texts.

Fields, Rick. 1984. *Chop Wood, Carry Water*. New York: TarcherPerigee.

Fischer, Zoketsu Norman. May 23, 2008. "On Being a Priest" at: www.everydayzen.org/teachings/2008/being-priest/

Fischer, Norman and Susan Moon. 2016. *What is Zen?* Boston, MA: Shambhala.

Hanh, Thich Nhat. 2006. *Understanding Our Mind*. Berkeley, CA: Parallax Press.

Kapleau, Phillip. 1965. *The Three Pillars of Zen*. Boston: Beacon Press.

Khema, Ayya. 1987. *Being Nobody, Going Nowhere*. Somerville, MA: Wisdom Press.

McGilchrist, Iain. 2009. *The Master and His Emissary*. New Haven and London: Yale University Press.

Norton, Edwina. "Both," *Passager*. 2007 Poetry Contest Journal edition. Baltimore, MD: United Book Press, 2007.

Seng-Ts'an, Zen Patriarch in China. (6th C.) "Hsin Hsin Ming" poem found at http://www.selfdiscoveryportal.com/cmSengTsan.htm.

Smith, Rodney. 2010. *Stepping Out of Self-Deception*. Boston, MA: Shambhala.

Tuchman, Bruce. 1965. *Forming, Storming, Norming, and Performing—Understanding the Stages of Team Formation* at https://www.mindtools.com/pages/article/newLDR_86.htm.

Watson, Burton. 1993. Tr. *The Zen Teachings of Master Lin-Chi*. Boston & London: Shambhala.

Watts, Alan. 1957. *The Way of Zen*. New York: Pantheon Books.

Weller, Francis. 2015. *The Wild Edge of Sorrow*. Berkeley, CA: North Atlantic Books.

Winnicott, D.W. 1971. *Playing and Reality*. New York: Basic Books.

About the Author

Edwina Norton is a painter, published poet, and peace activist. She has practiced Soto Zen Buddhism in California, Japan, and Washington state for fifty years. As an ordained Zen priest, she supports new and continuing lay practice students at Red Cedar Zen Community in Bellingham, Washington. She holds a B.A. and M.A. degree in English literature, has taught the subject on the high school and college levels, and has had a long career in organizational development.